INTEGRATION AND COMMUNITY BUILDING
IN EASTERN EUROPE

INTEGRATION AND COMMUNITY BUILDING
IN EASTERN EUROPE

Jan F. Triska, series editor

The German Democratic Republic
Arthur M. Hanhardt, Jr.

The Polish People's Republic
James F. Morrison

The Development of Socialist Yugoslavia
M. George Zaninovich

The People's Republic of Albania
Nicholas C. Pano

The Czechoslovak Socialist Republic
Zdenek Suda

The Socialist Republic of Rumania
Stephen Fischer-Galati

THE
CZECHOSLOVAK
SOCIALIST
REPUBLIC

ZDENEK SUDA

THE JOHNS HOPKINS PRESS

Baltimore

FOREWORD

This monograph on the Czechoslovak Socialist Republic by Professor Zdenek Suda is an empirical analysis and a case study of the relations Czechoslovakia has had with the other states ruled by Communist parties. As in the other studies in this series—on the U.S.S.R., Communist China, North Korea, Outer Mongolia, and the German Democratic Republic, and so on*—the focus here is on one country Czechoslovakia—as a political unit interacting with the other communist party states. It is not an isolated descriptive study of a communist-ruled country, the Czechoslovak Socialist Republic; instead, it is a study of Czechoslovakia as a unit *within* the communist party-state system, a part of a collective, systematic intellectual effort to assess empirically the scope, rate, and direction of integration among the states ruled by communist parties. This is why Professor Suda's focus of attention is that behavior and data of Czechoslovakia relevant to integration and

* The first four monographs in this series were published in the Hoover Institution Studies Series, *Integration and Community Building Among the Fourteen Communist Party-States*: Glenn D. Paige, *The Korean People's Democratic Republic;* Robert A. Rupen, *The Mongolian People's Republic*; Vernon V. Aspaturian, *The Soviet Union in the World Communist System*; Dennis J. Doolin and Robert C. North, *The Chinese People's Republic* (all 1966).

community formation with its neighbors and friends in the East.

Professor Suda rightly points out that Czechoslovakia holds a particularly significant place in the communist party-state system. Because of the high degree of economic development reached in Czechoslovakia prior to the seizure of power by the Communists, its democratic past and experience, its tradition of socialist and trade union movements, and a communist party sophisticated by its development and growth in a parliamentary setting, Czechoslovak communism has traveled a path different from the other ruling parties. "It was in Czechoslovakia that the basic tenets of dialectic and historical materialism were put to the test for the first time in an 'economically mature' environment postulated by Marx and Engels. By virtue of this particular background, Czechoslovakia appeared as a unique social, political, and economic laboratory. The results of the communist experiment there could be interpreted as a validity test of the Marxist doctrine, i.e., a testimony to the correctness of the Marxist interpretation of socioeconomic processes as well as the accuracy of the Marxist historical prognoses."

This statement, written by Dr. Suda before the invasion of Czechoslovakia, sounds almost prophetic. The Warsaw Pact armies did not, and could not, change the political development in Czechoslovakia. They just slowed down and postponed the inevitable. But they did prove, once and for all, the limits of communism as a thought, movement, and organization. By brutally suppressing the development of creative, socialist democracy in Czechoslovakia, the occupation forces suppressed genuine, voluntaristic maintenance, growth, and greater union of the world communist movement everywhere.

Like the other authors in this series, Zdenek Suda uses the concept of integration to describe such co-operative behavior where co-ordination—systems of information and adjustment of courses of action—is the efficient basis for joint action leading to a common goal. If all relevant units of the system are so involved, he speaks of integrated behavior. If most are involved, he speaks of extensive integration; and so on. A system may thus be integrated or not in a variety of ways, depending on the number and effectiveness of involved units.

In addition, a system may be integrated at the top level of authority, or it may be integrated on subordinate levels. The authority, furthermore, may be based essentially on coercion, or it may stem essentially from consensus. Which of these variables is more conducive to integrated behavior? Under what circumstances, when, and to what ends?

Zdenek Suda systematically tries to answer these questions by examining closely the data he has painstakingly collected. He discusses integration of Czechoslovakia into the communist party-state system both as a *condition* in which he found Czechoslovakia as well as a *process*—Czechoslovakia becoming integrated into the system.

Like the other authors in the series, Professor Suda attempts first to identify the statistical data potentially conducive to integration—in this case, Czechoslovakia's ecological-physical factors, its demographic structure, social system, degree of autonomy, and dependence upon other states. Next he discusses the *pre-entry* period, giving an analytical description of Czechoslovakia before it became a communist party state. This period is defined by the interwar development—the First Republic, Munich, World War II, and the "Bridge" episode after the war—which provides the descriptive baseline for the study. The *entry* and *post-entry* years are broken down into four distinct periods—intensive socialist development, the post-Stalin era, the period before the great change, and the liberalization before the Soviet invasion. For each of these periods the author examines various elements of the Czechoslovak communist-based society (e.g., the belief system, the political system, etc.) and attempts to detect salient changes in them. In addition, Suda discusses the dramatic turn of events starting with the Soviet occupation of Czechoslovakia.

This series is an intellectual product of many creative minds. In addition to the authors of the individual monographs—in this case, Professor Zdenek Suda—I would like to thank Professor David D. Finley of Stanford University and Colorado College for his original contribution and assistance and Mr. John Gallman of the Washington office of The Johns Hopkins University Press for his patient and sustained co-operation.

JAN F. TRISKA

Institute of Political Studies
Stanford University

CONTENTS

General Information

The Czechoslovak Socialist Republic
Československá Socialistická Republika

Area: 127,869 sq. km. (49,379 square miles)
Population: 14,271,547 (1967 preliminary figures)
Communist Party membership: 1,700,000 (round figure used by CPCS in Aug. 1968)
Population density: 111 per sq. km. (288 per square mile)
Population distribution: 35% in cities of 10,000 or more

Major Cities:	Population:
Praha (Prague)	1,025,000
Brno	330,000
Bratislava	272,000
Ostrava	265,000
Plzeň	141,000

Infant mortality: 23.7 per 1,000 live births
Physicians and dentists: 1 per 471 population (1966)

Illiteracy rate: nil in adult population
Higher education enrollment: 142,373 in 1966–67
Daily newspaper circulation: 97 copies per 1,000 population
Radio receivers: 333 per 1,000 population (1966)
TV receivers: 167 per 1,000 population (1966)
Radio stations: 80(1966); *TV stations:* 21(1966)
Gross national product: $60 billion in 1966
Rate of economic growth:
   7.8% annual average 1950–60
   3.7% annual average 1960–66
Industrial production index (1948=100): 341 (1966)
Railroad network: 13,330 km; transported in 1966, 560,700,000 passengers and 224,070 metric tons freight

International trade: $5,467 million (1966)

Currency: Czechoslovak crown (koruna)

The Czechoslovak Socialist Republic

INTRODUCTION

The Czechoslovak Socialist Republic holds a special place in the communist party-state system. The final alignment of Czechoslovakia with the system in February, 1948, signified the peak and at the same time the end of Soviet postwar expansion in Europe. Czechoslovakia was the only country in this region where the transformation from a Western-type, multiparty parliamentary government into that of a "people's democracy" happened abruptly, by a genuine coup d'état. Also, Czechoslovakia was the only modern industrialized nation to become communist, if we do not count that part of Germany which came under Soviet control following World War II. All the other party states had to begin their development on a level corresponding to that of the Soviet Union in 1917 and to carry out a communist revolution under "economically immature" conditions according to the blueprint set by Lenin.

It was in Czechoslovakia that the basic tenets of dialectic and historical materialism were put to the test for the first time in an "economically mature" environment postulated by Marx and Engels. By virtue of this particular background, Czechoslovakia appeared as a unique social, political, and economic laboratory. The results of the communist experiment there could be interpreted as a validity test of the Marxist doc-

1

trine, i.e., a testimony to the correctness of the Marxist interpretation of socioeconomic processes as well as the accuracy of the Marxist historical prognoses.

The entry of Czechoslovakia into the communist party-state system represented a challenge to the system. The degree of industrial development that had been reached prior to the seizure of power by the communists made Czechoslovakia a particularly heterogeneous element. All the other party states, with the sole exception of East Germany, had several common denominators, despite the diversity of their historical, cultural, economic, and social backgrounds. Most of all, they resembled one another in what they lacked: an adequate level of economic development, an experience in democratic government, a sufficiently long tradition of trade unionism and socialist movements, and last but not least, a communist party which had served its "apprenticeship years" in a parliamentary state.

Whereas almost all communist countries could see communism as a rapid way to industrialization and modernization which is the number one problem of underdeveloped nations, this incentive did not have much effect in Czechoslovakia. The Czechoslovak Communist Party could not hope to recruit many supporters motivated by a concern for the economic progress of their own country, except in the eastern, relatively less developed provinces. On the whole, the roots of Czechoslovak communism have been of a different kind than found in other East European states.

The distinctly different origin of the Czechoslovak communist movement remained visible throughout the twenty years of the Party's rule after 1948. It proved to be a serious obstacle to the development of integrative relationships with other communist party states, notably in the post-Stalinist period, when the policy of "vertical" integration through uniformity and imitation of the Soviet model was reversed and attempts were made at a "horizontal," more genuine kind of integration. The "de-Stalinization" and "liberalization" process in Czechoslovakia, which started relatively late and gained a strong momentum especially at the beginning of 1968, had its own dynamics, independent of the general trends within the communist party-state system. Through the experience of the "Czechoslovak Spring," which brought a change of social climate and institutional reforms reaching farther than any transformation so far observed in Central and Eastern Europe, Czechoslovakia became a distinctly separate element in the communist world. The dramatic conflict with the Soviet Union, in the form of a military intervention of the Warsaw Pact armies in August, 1968, slowed—and partly even stopped—the concrete program of the modification of Czechoslovak political and economic institutions, but it could not undo the fact that Czechoslovakia had already outgrown the framework of the communist party-state system.

We can expect that in the future the extent and the depth of the change which occurred in Czechoslovakia will become ever more patent. Unlike in similar situations hitherto observed in other communist countries, the reform movement and the political mobilization against Soviet interference affected the nation in its entirety, including the bulk of the communist party. The communist organization passed, virtually *en bloc*, into the national camp. The transformation of society accomplished during the short span of the "Prague Spring 1968" is of lasting nature. It is likely to defy, for a long time to come, the call for "normalization" coming from the Kremlin.

This challenge to the center of power of the system may move Soviet leaders to dangerous options—options which could further curtail the freedom of movement, or even threaten the independent existence of the Czechoslovak state, but which could in no case cure the corrosion afflicting the world communist movement. The unsuccessful history of communism in Czechoslovakia not only illustrates its inability to answer basic problems of an industrially advanced society but also indicates the poor chances of communist integration on international level.

1: THE PRE-ENTRY PERIOD

The Czechoslovak Socialist Republic forms the western outpost of the communist party-state system in Europe. Although the borders of East Germany extend, in certain parts, even farther west, the extreme position of Czechoslovakia is striking. It illustrates the discrepancy between the geographical concept of Eastern Europe and the political meaning of this term, generally accepted today. The capital of Czechoslovakia, Prague, for example, lies about 200 miles north west of Vienna, a city whose right to a place in the West European community nobody would dream to doubt; yet few seem to be disturbed by the fact that, in order to reach "Eastern Europe," a Viennese has to travel westward. On the other hand, if we consider the natural limits of Europe, without the actual political division, Czechoslovakia is situated literally in its heart.

In contrast with the situation existing before the Second World War, when Czechoslovakia had been a truly multinational state, the ethnic spectrum of the country was notably simplified after 1945 as a result of the transfer of the German minority and the exchange of population with Hungary. The two "nation-building" ethnic groups ("die Staatsvölker"), the Czechs and the Slovaks, constitute at present over 94 percent of all inhabitants.

5

Integration within a larger political or economic framework has never been a matter of pure theoretical speculation in Czechoslovakia; it has been a matter of experience. Even if this area's earlier history is by-passed and consideration of its past begins with more modern times, it can be pointed out that the three provinces of the present Republic—Bohemia, Moravia, and Slovakia—were components of the Austro-Hungarian Empire. It was on the ruins of this Empire that Czechoslovakia, like several other states in Central and Eastern Europe, was created in 1918.

The development and the ultimate fate of Austria-Hungary are an example of the sharp conflict between economic, "objective" forces striving toward an integration of the Danube region, and political and ethnic "subjective" forces opposing such a drive. Although the Habsburg Empire was an almost ideally self-contained economic unit, its ruling German-speaking minority failed to identify itself fully with the country. In spite of enjoying a privileged position of leadership within the state, most members of the German ethnic group felt more loyal to neighboring Germany and viewed an eventual incorporation of Austria-Hungary—or at least of its western half—into the German state as the most desirable solution.

These views were, of course, incompatible with the political aspirations of the non-German ethnic elements. Afraid of a possible "engulfment in the German sea," these peoples—the Czechs, the Poles, the Slovenes—looked for a support outside the Danube monarchy, mostly in Russia, France, or Italy. On the other hand, the policy of ruthless Magyarization pursued by the dominant Hungarian minority in the eastern part of the Empire estranged the populations of Slav and Rumanian origin from the idea of the Austro-

Hungarian state. Some of these ethnic groups eventually came to prefer the politically more tolerable, albeit economically disadvantageous, idea of unification with their racially and linguistically closer related neighbors: Serbia, Rumania, Russia. In a similar way, the Slovaks, seeing their very existence threatened, sought closer contact and support with their "next of kin" in the western part of the Empire, the Czechs; thus foundations were laid for the later reunion of both peoples in one state, Czechoslovakia. When, in 1914, the expansionist policies of the Vienna court, of which the majority of Austro-Hungarian citizenship disapproved, precipitated World War I, the inner contradictions finally tore apart one of the most "naturally" integrated political organisms in European history.[1]

The First Republic (1918–1938)

The disintegration of the Habsburg monarchy could not in itself efface geopolitical and geosocial realities in Central and Eastern Europe, least of all the mutual economic dependence of the peoples in the Danube region. As one of the successor states of Austria Hungary, Czechoslovakia thus inherited the latter's inner conflict caused by a propensity to economic integration within one area and a drive for political integration oriented toward a completely different area. Under the new conditions, this age-old conflict took new forms but did not lose much of its intensity.

Since its creation in 1918, Czechoslovakia has been also faced with serious problems of integration on the

[1] Robert A. Kann, *A Multinational Empire: Nationalism and National Reform in the Habsburg Monarchy 1848–1918* (F. A. Praeger: New York, 1950).

national level. Although the two nation-building ethnic groups, the Czechs and the Slovaks, represented an absolute majority of the population (about 66 percent), there were also important ethnic minorities—mainly German and Hungarian. To win over these minorities to the idea of the Czechoslovak state was a continuous challenge to the political leaders of the First Republic. Not until a forceful and dramatic solution of the minorities problem after World War II was imposed in the form of expulsion of the Sudeten German minority and a mass exchange of population with Hungary, did the nationalities issue cease to be of paramount importance.

On the other hand, the problem of relations between the Czechs and the Slovaks has proved to be chronic. It started with the necessity to integrate the western and the eastern provinces within the framework of the state. Before 1918, Bohemia and Moravia were parts of Austria and belonged to the most industrially developed and politically advanced regions of the Habsburg Empire; the eastern provinces, Slovakia and Ruthenia, were parts of the predominantly agrarian, semifeudal Hungary until the end of World War I.[2] As Slovakia was rapidly catching up with the general socioeconomic level in the Czech provinces, it became obvious that any durable solution of the Czecho-Slovak relationship could be found only in a federalist reconstruction of the state on federalist principles. However, the process of integration has been considerably retarded by strong centralist tendencies on the Czech side. This centralism has been the principal reason for the slow progress of integration on the national

[2] This province, sometimes called also Carpatho-Ukraine, was lost to the Soviets in 1945.

level during the twenty years of the First Republic and why no systematic attempt at the solution of the "Slovak problem" has been made until 1968.

Even after the dissolution of the Habsburg Empire, voices could be heard advocating a close co-operation, if not an integration or "re-integration," of these countries—successor states. On the other hand, old ethnic resentments represented strong centrifugal factors which have prevailed. An attempt to reunite the ethnic remainder of Hungary with the German-speaking remnant of Austria ("Deutsch-Österreich") under the scepter of the former Emperor Charles I. was thwarted, in 1921, by a joint action of Czechoslovakia, Rumania, and Yugoslavia, who saw in it the first step towards the restoration of the much hated Austro-Hungarian "prison of nations."

The fear of an eventual Habsburg comeback and the concern about Hungary's demands for restitution of large parts of territories which had belonged to it before the Treaty of Trianon in 1920 led to the creation of the "Little Entente" in the early twenties. Initially this was a mere military alliance of Czechoslovakia, Rumania, and Yugoslavia; gradually, it developed into a system of political and diplomatic co-operation. Towards the end of the inter-war period, efforts were made to give the "Little Entente" economic significance, in the form of customs agreements, simplified border formalities, common railway freight tariffs, etc. The alliance fulfilled its primary objective, as neither Hungary nor Austria, whether taken separately or with combined forces, constituted a serious threat to the existence of the "Little Entente" countries. However, after 1933, when the actual danger to Czechoslovakia came from Hitler's Germany, the "Little Entente" as such was not able to cope with this danger unless taken as part of a broader defense system, including at least one of the great European powers. Although Czechoslovakia had been allied, since 1925, to France by a Mutual Assistance Treaty, a link between this pact and the "Little Entente" was neither automatic nor without complications. Serious complications arose after 1935, when the Soviet Union became party to the French-Czechoslovak Pact. The allies of Czechoslovakia in the "Little Entente," primarily Rumania, considered the U.S.S.R. a potential enemy. Nevertheless, the "Little Entente" was a remarkable attempt to integrate a part of the Danubian region at that time.

It was characteristic of the deep and inveterate economic and political contradictions prevailing in Central and Eastern Europe that the trade relations between Czechoslovakia and her partners in the "Little Entente" had never achieved the intensity and frequency of the trade relations with her potential political rivals. A good example is the development of economic co-operation with Austria.[3] The case of Germany is even more remarkable. Germany had been, throughout the period of the First Republic, Czechoslovakia's most important trade partner. These relations did not change much even after the seizure of power by Hitler, although the Nazi regime did not dissimulate its intention to destroy Czechoslovakia, should a favorable international situation arise.[4] On the other hand, the economic ties with France, with which Czechoslovakia had been politically and militarily associated from the very beginning, were quite

[3] Cf. *Statistická ročenka Československé republiky* ("The Statistical Yearbook of the Czechoslovak Republic," hereafter referred to as *The Statistical Yearbook*) *1938*, p. 138.

[4] Cf. *The Statistical Yearbook 1934*, pp. 130–31 and *The Statistical Yearbook 1938*, p. 138.

loose. The mutual trade of the two countries could not compare to that of Czechoslovakia and Germany, nor did it reach the level of the turnover between Czechoslovakia and Austria.[5] The discrepancy between Czechoslovak economic interests and the concern for the country's military security was even more obvious in the relationship with the Soviet Union: The foreign trade between the two countries, practically nonexistent before the conclusion of the Czechoslovak-Soviet Treaty, remained negligible after its signature in 1935 and during all the remaining years of the inter-war period.[6]

Among various proposals for European integration of the time, the "Paneuropa" movement, founded by Count Coudenhove-Kalergi in 1923, enjoyed support from leading Czechoslovak politicians (especially the first president of the Republic, Thomas G. Masaryk) and was viewed with sympathy by Czech and Slovak elites.[7] However, the relevant strata of the Czechoslovak population continued to be aware of the fact that integration trends in Central and Eastern Europe ran opposite to political interests and military engagements. This knowledge rendered them rather skeptical about the practicability of the "Paneuropa" program.

An observer today should not overlook the fact that it was inevitable for Czechoslovakia to suffer prolonged contradictions in her foreign relations. The First Republic—"the only positive outcome of World War I" as H. G. Wells termed it[8]—was an outpost of democ-

---

[5] Cf. *The Statistical Yearbook 1938*, p. 138.

[6] Cf. *The Statistical Yearbook 1934*, pp. 130–31 and *The Statistical Yearbook 1938*, p. 138.

[7] Richard Coudenhove-Kalergi, *An Idea Conquers the World* (London: Hutchinson, 1953).

[8] Cf. H. G. Wells, *The Outline of History* (London: Cassell, 1951).

11

racy in the heart of Europe that could hardly entertain perfect relationships with its fascist and semi-fascist neighbors, unless it denied the very ideals upon which it had been established. Moreover, many of these neighbors had substantial territorial claims on Czechoslovakia or even worked for its destruction, like Germany after 1933. Thus the prevalence of political and military criteria over economic ones, to the detriment of all parties concerned, was for Czechoslovakia not a matter of choice but of necessity.

Munich and World War II

The sacrifices the young state had to bear and the risks to which it was exposed could have been justified only as long as the two main architects of the established order in Central and Eastern Europe after the First World War, England and France, were able and willing to uphold the results of their diplomatic work. However, the Western powers, neither quite sure nor unanimous about their policy on Germany while Germany still had a democratic government, embarked upon the "appeasement" road as soon as the National Socialist Party seized power. The "appeasement" reached its peak during the "Czechoslovak crisis" in autumn 1938, with France refusing to honor her signature on the 1925 Mutual Assistance Treaty, in a situation which was a clear-cut *casus foederis*: Hitler's ultimatum on the cession of Czechoslovak border territories was tantamount to unprovoked aggression for which the Treaty had provided. At the same time, a clause in the complementary tripartite Pact, concluded in 1935 by France, Czechoslovakia, and Soviet Russia, made help by the Soviet Union dependent on how the given situation would be interpreted by France, which enabled the Soviet government to score an easy propaganda success. The chief Soviet delegate to the League of Nations in Geneva, Mr. Litvinov, claimed during the crisis that the Soviet Union was willing to assist Czechoslovakia but that it was prevented from doing so by the stipulations of the 1935 Pact. On the basis of this inexpensive gesture, the Czechoslovak Communist Party was able to collect enormous propaganda dividends for many years to come.[9]

The Munich Conference in September, 1938, satisfied fully the demands of the Third Reich and led, eventually, not only to the disintegration of Czechoslovakia but also to the ruin of the political system set up in Europe by the victors of World War I.[10] The Czechoslovak leaders had to recognize that the structure of international relations upon which the security of Czechoslovakia had rested since 1918 lacked solid foundations. A last-hour attempt to accommodate the aggressive neighbor did not succeed, less than half a year after Munich, Hitler occupied the remainder of Bohemia and Moravia and transformed that section into a German "protectorate." Profiting by the unsolved problem of Czecho-Slovak relations, Germany established, with the aid of extreme nationalist Slovak elements, a puppet state in Slovakia, where large territories in the south, inhabited chiefly by population of Hungarian ethnic origin, had already been lost to Hungary, following the arbitration of the Vienna Conference in November, 1938. As of March, 1939, Czechs and Slovaks found themselves integrated within the system of Greater Germany. Although this solution did

---

[9] Cf. John Bennet Wheeler, *Munich—Prologue to Tragedy* (London: Macmillan, 1963). Hubert Ripka, *Munich and After* (London: Gollancz, 1939).

[10] *Ibid.*

not contradict the "natural" trends toward economic partnership in Central Europe, it was even less satisfactory than any earlier arrangement because it denied all political aspirations of many generations and all great traditions of the nation.

The effect of the experience of Munich upon the politically relevant strata of the Czechoslovak population can hardly be exaggerated, as it produced an important shift in Czechoslovakia's image of its position in Europe. All through World War II, political leaders at home and in exile were seeking more reliable safeguards of national independence for the future reconstituted Czechoslovakia than the guarantees once given by the West had been. Though this concern did not make Czechoslovak political elites become communist or even necessarily pro-communist, it made them accept a future alliance with the Soviet Union as unavoidable. This lowered, to a large extent, Czechoslovakia's defenses against communism. Adroit communist propaganda, building upon the widely recognized importance for Czechoslovakia of Soviet assistance and presenting the Communist Party as identical with the Soviet state, could later stigmatize any polemic against the CPCS as an "anti-Soviet move, detrimental to the interests of the nation."[11]

The roots of the ultimate integration of Czechoslovakia with the communist party-state system can thus be traced as far back as Munich. However, important events during World War II contributed even more to this integration. The first formal political act which indicated the basic change in the orientation of Czechoslovak foreign policy was the Czechoslovak-Soviet

[11] Klement Gottwald, *Spisy* ("Collected Works") (Prague: Státní nakladatelství politické literatury, 1956) vol. XII, pp. 13–25.

Friendship and Mutual Assistance Treaty, signed in Moscow in 1943 by the Soviet Union and by the Czechoslovak exile government in London. The other event which determined the course of the post-war development in Czechoslovakia was the "division of spheres of influence," agreed upon by the Great Powers at the Yalta Conference, in February 1945. Although the U.S.S.R. had given a formal pledge to respect the political will of the peoples in Central and Eastern Europe and to allow them "to establish a form of government of their choice," the informal delimitation of the spheres of influence in Europe, tacitly accepted at this conference, gave Stalin a chance to impose communist regimes everywhere in the Soviet sphere. This sphere corresponded roughly to the zone reserved for occupation by the Red Army. Czechoslovakia was included in the zone.[12] The fact that, as the war approached its end, American troops were able to penetrate some 80 miles deep into Czechoslovak territory could not change the political effect of the Yalta decisions. The only politically and psychologically relevant alternative—namely a possible liberation of Prague by the Americans—was vetoed by the Soviets.[13]

The Communist Party of Czechoslovakia

The Communist Party of Czechoslovakia—CPCS— came into existence in 1921, after a split in the Czecho-

[12] Cf. Edward Beneš, *Memoirs* (London: Allen & Unwin, 1954), pp. 252–53. Cf. also Snell-Pogue-Delzell-Lensen, *The Meaning of Yalta* (Baton Rouge: Louisiana State University Press, 1956), pp. 119–26.

[13] Cf. Dwight D. Eisenhower, *Crusade in Europe* (Garden City: Garden City Books, 1952), p. 460; *cf.* also the memoirs of Gen. George Patton, as quoted by the Czechoslovak Service of the Voice of America, Washington, D.C., at the eve of the 20th anniversary of Patton's death.

15

slovak Social Democratic organization. All that time, the socialist movement in Czechoslovakia could look back upon almost half a century of work and struggle. Socialist traditions had earlier beginnings in Bohemia and Moravia than in Slovakia, although even there a socialist party had existed before World War I.[14]

The so-called Social Democratic Left, nucleus of the future Communist Party, had a strong following among the socialist rank and file.[15] In 1921, the year of its foundation, the CPCS could claim no less than 350,000 registered members. The Party reached the maximum of influence on the parliamentary level with the election of 1925, the first election in which it appeared separately on the ballot. It received 13.3 percent of the vote and obtained 41 seats out of 300. The highest proportion of communist voting was recorded in the ethnically mixed regions on the Hungarian and Polish border, though this fact in itself cannot substantiate the interpretation by some scholars of communism in Czechoslovakia as an expression of discontent among ethnic minorities.[16] At the time of the 1925 election, however, the Party membership was down to 280,000. It dropped even more sharply in the following five years, when a series of intra-party conflicts and

[14] Cf. Miloš Gosiorovsky, *Dejiny slovenského robotnickeho hnutia 1848–1918* ("History of the Slovak Workers' Movement 1848–1918") (Slovenské vydavatelstvo politickej literatúry, Bratislava 1956), pp. 175–89.

[15] Cf. Pavel Reiman et al., *Dějiny komunistické strany Československa* ("The History of the Communist Party of Czechoslovakia"), (Prague: Státní nakladatelství politické literatury, 1961), pp. 143–54; *cf.* also William E. Griffith, *Communism in Europe*, volume 2, part 2 (authors Zdenek Eliáš and Jaroslav Netík), pp. 167–68.

[16] Richard V. Burks, *Dynamics of Communism in Eastern Europe* (Princeton: Princeton University Press, 1961).

chronic ideological crises was responsible for a setback in the 1929 election when the CPCS polled only 10.2 percent of the vote and kept 30 seats in the Parliament. The Party organization was almost wiped out early in 1930, when there were only 30,000 communists in Czechoslovakia holding a membership card. The situation of the movement improved again after 1930, though its effective strength could no longer compare with that of 1925, let alone with the period immediately after its constitution in 1921. The depression years 1929–1933, which hit Czechoslovakia particularly severely,[17] brought practically no benefit to the CPCS. In the last parliamentary election during the First Republic in 1935, the communist vote increased by only 0.1 percent. There was a more perceptible swell of communist suffrage among the Czech population during the municipal election in May, 1938, after the Party, in accordance with the general policy line of the Comintern prevailing at that time, had displayed an at least verbally resolute anti-Nazi attitude.[18]

Among all communist parties in Central and Eastern Europe, including the German and Austrian parties, the Communist Party of Czechoslovakia was the only one to enjoy an uninterrupted and openly legal political activity within a democratic parliamentary system

[17] Czechoslovakia, at the lowest ebb of depression in 1929–1933, had, among its 14 million population, 920,182 unemployed. The per capita unemployment figure was thus comparable to that reached in the United States (13 million jobless in a nation of 150 million); cf. *The Statistical Yearbook 1936*.

[18] The municipal elections in May, 1938, ranked the Communist Party among the first three parties in many industrial centers such as Plzeň, Prague, and Ostrava; cf. Kiesing, *Archiv der Gegenwart* ("Contemporary Archives"), Berlin & Frankfurt, 1938, vol. 1, pp. 3569 and 3578.

all through the interwar period. This does not mean, of course, that the years of apprenticeship in a democratic system of government made the Czechoslovak communists appreciate the values of a free society better than did their comrades who had to suffer all possible hardships of illegal underground work and persecution in the neighboring countries.[19] From the beginning, the program of the CPCS was fundamentally revolutionary; it refused not only the "bourgeois-democratic" regime of Czechoslovakia, but also the Czechoslovak state as such. The communists claimed the First Republic was "an artificial creation of the imperialist powers, part of the legacy of the predatory peace dictate of Versailles."[20] Destruction of this state appeared to the Communist Party as a primary condition toward improvement of international relations in Central Europe. These views were strikingly similar to those of various radical right-wing elements among the ethnic minorities in Czechoslovakia, especially among the Germans, but they were not a mere reflection of revolutionary nihilism. The Party hoped to attract thus into its own sails the wind of dissatisfaction of the

[19] It was not incidental that communist parties in the two "classical" Western democracies, England and France, were, until recently, the most dogmatic ones. The Czechoslovak Party, which found itself in a similar situation, had to act very cautiously, because any perceptible move towards a more liberal line would have brought the Party dangerously close to the powerful current of Czechoslovak democratic socialism. Cf. Zdenek Suda, "Il Enigma Ceccoslovaco" ("The Czechoslovak Enigma"), *Tempo Presente* (Rome), 1963, No. 8.

[20] Cf. the Protocols of the First Congress of the Communist Party of Czechoslovakia (Prague, February 2–February 5, 1923), the Protocols of the Second Congress of the CPCS (Prague, October 31–November 4, 1924), as well as those of the Fifth Congress of the Communist International in Moscow (June 17–July 8, 1924).

minority groups. The ethnic irredentism in communist politics was not an end in itself, but one of disintegrative elements to be exploited. The fact is that the Party organization has always been strictly centralist and has never allowed for any autonomy on either ethnic or regional levels.[21]

When, in the early twenties, several improvised "revolutionary" actions failed and it became obvious that no violent change of the existing order was to be expected in the near future, the Party put more stress on the "enlightenement work among the masses" and on "social movement" or "economic struggle," namely, wage bargaining through communist trade unions, etc., but its basically negative attitude toward the State remained unchanged. The Czechoslovak communists, for many years, also refused to cooperate with any other political party, most of all with the Social Democrats, whom they called "traitors of the working class" and "Social-Fascists." Only in the second half of the thirties, under the impact of the Popular Front experiment in France, did the communists leaders begin to recommend a "joint action of the Left." These proposals did not meet with a warm reception on the part of the Socialists and, consequently, a Popular Front government has never become a reality in Czechoslovakia.

The development of the policies of the Communist Party of Czechoslovakia was parallel to the general line of the Comintern, with which the CPCS had been affiliated from the very beginning. The relations with

[21] Separate ethnic units of the communist movement which had come into existence after the split in the Czechoslovak Social Democratic Party were fused in a unique centralized party organization as early as in Nov. 1921. Cf. Pavel Reiman, *The History of the CPCS*, pp. 165–74.

the Soviet Union were equally close or even closer, since the CPCS was sponsored by the U.S.S.R., as all communist parties between the two world wars were. It was under the impact of the Bolshevik revolution that the Czechoslovak Socialist movement split. The Communist Party thus represented a distinctly foreign body in the political life of the First Republic, integrated within an external organization and obedient to an alien power center. Its foreign character became even more accentuated as Stalin succeeded in transforming the Comintern into a direct instrument of the Soviet foreign policy. The subservience of the CPCS leadership to Moscow could hardly be seriously questioned at that time. Regular purges—the most conspicuous among which had been the "bolshevization" of the Party in 1929—made it possible for the leaders devoted to Kremlin to dispose of all of the more independent-thinking elements among the cadres.[22]

Although relatively sudden, the change in the attitude of the Communist Party toward the Czechoslovak Republic, manifested by the adoption of an anti-German and patriotic line, was in agreement with the overall trend of Soviet foreign relations. During the "Czechoslovak crisis" in September, 1938, the CPCS took a firm anti-Nazi stand and denounced the "traitorous and capitulationist position of the bourgeois government" without, however, suggesting an alternative course except for vague hints at a possibility of securing Soviet assistance.

The right-wing government of the post-Munich

---

[22] *Příspěvky k dějinám KSČ* ("Essays on the History of the CPCS"), published by the Institute of the Party History in Prague, no. 5/1961, May 1961; cf. also Pavel Reiman, *The History of the CPCS*, pp. 249–69.

Czechoslovakia dissolved the Communist Party at the end of 1938. The communist movement, to which this blow was no surprise, went underground in a fairly orderly and disciplined way. The most prominent communist leaders, headed by the Secretary General Klement Gottwald, chose exile in Moscow. Further problems arose for the Party after the final dismemberment of Czechoslovakia in March, 1939, whereby the illegal Communist Party found itself split into two parts: one, in the Protectorate Bohemia and Moravia, annexed to the German *Reich*; the other, in the Slovak puppet state. Although Moscow tried very hard to maintain unity of the organization, in order to keep better control over it, very soon a separate underground Communist Party of Slovakia was set up. Thus the seeds of the future conflict between the centralist governing body of the CPCS and the Slovak nationalists were sown.

Another test of cohesion of the underground communist organizations was the signing of the Soviet-German Pact in August, 1939. Although some intellectuals and Party functionaries protested—among them the Slovak Communist leader Vlado Clementis—the bulk of the illegal organizations survived this shock without much damage. During the first two years of the Second World War, while the Soviets still were declaring the war to be an "imperialist and plutocratic venture," the underground CPCS cells faithfully observed the instructions from Moscow. The Czechoslovak national liberation movement at home and abroad was rejected by the communists as "irresponsible war-mongery" in the service of "aggressive Western imperialism."[23] After the German attack on the

[23] Cf. the resolution of the Executive Committee of the Communist Party of Czechoslovakia of December 15, 1940, as quoted in Beneš, *Memoirs*, pp. 160–61.

Soviet Union in June, 1941, the Party adopted a different view of the war, but the communist leaders, both in Czechoslovakia and in exile, continued to shun cooperation with the non-communist anti-Nazi resistance groups.

It was only late in 1943 that the first concrete negotiations took place between the representatives of the Czechoslovak national liberation movement and the communist leadership. The most important talks were held in Moscow, at the occasion of the signing of the Soviet-Czechoslovak Treaty of Friendship, Mutual Assistance and Postwar Cooperation, in December, 1943. The CPCS did not take any direct part in this diplomatic act, but the delegation of the Czechoslovak exile government in London, presided over by Eduard Beneš, met with the Party leadership upon an explicit recommendation from the Kremlin. It was agreed that the communists would be included in the postwar government coalition on the basis of parity with the other political parties. The agreement contained several decisions which later played an important role in the incorporation of Czechoslovakia into the communist party-state system, including nationalization of key industries; confiscation of the property of traitors and collaborators; transfer of the German ethnic minority and resettlement of the border areas; extensive land reform; and a "simplification" of the political parties system by disqualification and exclusion of the parties which had participated in the post-Munich government.[24]

In Slovakia, the noncommunist democratic underground groups concluded a so-called "Christmas Agreement" with the Communist Party of Slovakia in De-

[24] Cf. Eduard Beneš, *Memoirs*, p. 98; pp. 268–75.

cember, 1943. This document laid down the principles upon which the political life in the future Slovakia was to be organized within the framework of a reconstituted Czechoslovakia. The Christmas Agreement found its first practical application during the Slovak uprising in August, 1944. The tactics used by the communists in the course of the uprising gave their noncommunist partners a foretaste of the postwar coalition with the CPCS. Slovak communists, who were in absolute minority at the beginning of the revolt, succeeded finally in gaining the upper hand.[25] At the same time, the experience of an independently conducted revolutionary action increased the self-confidence in the ranks of the Communist Party of Slovakia and added considerably to the tension between the leaders in Slovakia and the CPCS leadership in Moscow.

The "Slovak problem" within the communist movement became increasingly serious in the first months after the liberation. The Slovak Party groups, strengthened by years of self-reliance in underground work, refused to submit to the rigid centralist organization according to the pre-war pattern which the Party chiefs were determined to maintain. In order to pacify the Slovak nationalist currents, a compromise was worked out in 1945. The Communist Party of Slovakia was included in the CPCS as an autonomous body, while the Communist Party of Czechoslovakia remained not only the supreme organization in the state, but also the basis of local organizations in the two western provinces, Bohemia and Moravia. This solution was inconsistent and awkward, establishing a kind of "asymmetric cen-

---

[25] Cf. Mikuláš Ferjenčík: "Open Letter to the Editor of the Czechoslovak Quarterly *Svědectví* on the Slovak National Uprising 1944," *Svědectví* vol. VI, no. 22 (Paris, Oct., 1963), 149–54.

tralism" as there were no corresponding autonomous Party organizations in the Czech regions. Although it served later as a model for the legislative and administrative structure of liberated Czechoslovakia, the communist approach to the problem of integration on the national level did not prove fruitful and aggravated the issue considerably. Both the Party and the state were deeply affected by this failure to reconcile the interests of Czechs and Slovaks for many years to come.

When the leadership returned from exile and started to reorganize the membership, they could count upon a "hard core" of some forty thousand communists who had remained faithful to the Party in spite of the war, occupation, and persecution. It was a number which no other political party could match, and it gave the CPCS an enormous advantage over its coalition partners. Moreover, the military authorities in the territories liberated by the Red Army very often helped the communist functionaries in their work and deliberately impeded the setting up of local groups of other political orientation.

However, these were not the only circumstances by which the CPCS could profit. The exclusion of all conservative and rightist parties and movements from the national life left large segments of the population politically "homeless," especially in the Czech countryside which, until 1939, had been the domain of the Agrarian (Republican) Party. A certain portion of the Agrarian membership chose the Populist Party, corresponding to Christian Democratic parties in Western Europe, but many former Agrarians were repelled by the relatively pronounced Catholic character of the Populist movement. Still less numerous were the Agrarians who joined the People's Socialist Party, which

24

appealed to the mentality of the middle-class urban elector rather than to that of a peasant. The situation was different in Slovakia, where the Slovak Democratic Party could absorb the bulk of the adherents of the dissolved pre-war parties. There, the communists built their strength chiefly at the cost of the socialists, whose party was thus almost wiped out. In Bohemia and Moravia, however, an apparently paradoxical development took place: Many small holders, cottagers, as well as well-to-do farmers joined the communist organizations which seemed attractive to them chiefly because the Communist Party controlled the Ministry of Agriculture and through it the distribution of land confiscated from the Sudeten Germans and pro-Nazi collaborators. Moreover, not a negligible percentage of new CPCS members was recruited among the extremists of all shades and, last but not least, individuals whose record was tarnished by collaboration with the Nazis and who sought in the Party a protection from a possible legal prosecution. Finally, crude profiteers who were trying to use membership in the most powerful party to their economic advantage were not rare in the communist ranks. Before 1945 was over, the state-wide membership figure for the CPCS surpassed one million. The Communist Party became a true mass organization at that time.

The "Bridge" Episode

The conditions favorable to a complete communist take-over were thus, to a large extent, given before Czechoslovakia was re-established as an independent country. Upon their return home from exile, many noncommunist politicians came to realize that, instead of a true liberation, they had brought to their people an "almost accomplished communist revolution."[26]

The political order in the immediate postwar period was defined in the Košice Program, which the Communist Party and the noncommunist leaders signed in April, 1945, in Košice, the provisory seat of the Czechoslovak Government in Eastern Slovakia. In addition to the concretely defined policy aims which were based upon the previous talks between the London exile group and the communists, the Košice Program provided for a mode of co-operation among the political parties in the National Assembly and in the Cabinet of Ministers. All parties were to participate in the "National Front of the Urban and Rural Working People"—the future government coalition. There was no provision for an eventual parliamentary opposition, though the text did not explicitly preclude its existence. The Košice Program contained one more important limitation of classical parliamentary democracy: It did not allow the renewal of any pre-war political parties except of those represented in the National Front. Including the Communist Party of Slovakia, which presented itself separately in the election campaign, there were seven authorized political parties in the whole country.[27]

[26] Cf. the lecture given by Jaroslav Stránský, former Minister of Justice and Minister of Education in the 1945–1948 governments, at the Eduard Beneš Institute in London. *Publications of the Eduard Beneš Institute* (London, 1951).

[27] The seven authorized political parties in post-war Czechoslovakia were: Communist Party of Czechoslovakia (operating only in the Czech provinces of Bohemia and Moravia); Communist Party of Slovakia (in Slovakia only); Democratic Party (in Slovakia only); Slovak Labor Party (in Slovakia only); People's Socialist Party (in Czech provinces only); Populist Party (Christian Democratic) (in Czech provinces only); Czechoslovak

Although these limitations constituted part of the communist power strategy for the ultimate seizure of all control, the noncommunist parties wholeheartedly supported them, hoping that they themselves would profit from this political "closed shop." They also fully approved and even tried to outbid the chauvinist radicalism of the Communist Party in the matter of forcible transfer of ethnic minorities and of "building the new Republic as a purely national state of Czechs and Slovaks." The "bourgeois" partners of the CPCS, furthermore, remained silent—or protested too timidly or too late—in the face of countless injustices and violations of the basic legal principles, committed during the investigation and the trials of collaborators and other "unreliable" elements. They were to pay dearly for their short-sightedness.

In the eyes of the noncommunist members of the National Front, the philosophy underlying the Košice Program was that of "active co-existence," though the term had not yet been known in 1945. It reflected the changed position of Czechoslovakia in a changed Europe and was supposed to be more than mere tactics for a transitory period. The noncommunist majority sought to preserve a democratic and independent Czechoslovakia within the Soviet power orbit. Czechoslovakia was to be a loyal ally to the Soviet Union but was not expected to sever her links with the West. As it was formulated by Eduard Beneš, President of the

---

Social Democratic Party (in Czech provinces only). After the elections of 1946, the Slovak Labor Party merged with the Social Democratic Party but a new Slovak party was constituted, namely the Liberty Party, so that the number of parties remained constant.

Republic, the renewed Czechoslovak state was to become "a bridge between the West and the East."[28]

The concept of the "bridge" was more difficult to carry out in practice than its supporters were willing to admit. The simultaneous embedding of Czechoslovakia in the Soviet sphere of influence and the maintaining of economic, cultural, and political bonds between Czechoslovakia and the West required two basic conditions. First of all, the European and the world siutation and especially the relationship between the two superpowers, the United States and the Soviet Union, would have had to be at least a mutual tolerance. However, the international climate in the postwar years was too tense and the positions of the two big rivals too sharply polarized. Second, the Communist Party of Czechoslovakia would have had to give up the desire to seize absolute control. This turned out to be very difficult for the Communist Party because, as a revolutionary organization, it naturally tended to strive for unlimited power while the conditions appeared extraordinarily favorable for it.

The precarious nature of the "bridge" concept was clearly exposed after the election in May, 1946. During this election, the Communist Party polled 36 percent of the vote, gaining in certain areas, particularly in those border regions where the German-speaking popu-

---

[28] Cf. Eduard Beneš, *Memoirs*, pp. 281–86. The idea of the "Bridge," implied by the author in the conclusion, was later formulated explicitly when Beneš made several public statements on the subject of Czechoslovakia's position in the postwar world. However, the metaphor used by President Beneš was not always accepted without reserve by his noncommunist collaborators. For instance, Minister of Foreign Affairs Jan Masaryk used to say that he did not like to think of Czechoslovakia as a bridge: "Bridges are here to be trod upon!"

lation had been expelled, as much as over 50 percent.[29] It was obvious that the outcome of the election would render the CPCS less willing than ever to renounce or to suspend its claim for absolute power.

One year later, an important event showed that the general trend of international politics was highly unfavorable to the "bridge" experiment. Although Czechoslovakia had at first accepted, by a unanimous decision of the Council of Ministers, on July 7, 1947, the invitation of the U.S. Secretary of State George C. Marshall to participate in the European Recovery Program (Marshall Plan), an energetic intervention of the Soviet Union forced her last-minute withdrawal from the preparatory conference in Paris.[30] This incident demonstrated, in a most revealing way, the extremely narrow margin of operation available to the noncommunist majority in the government. On these terms the "bridge between East and West" was bound to remain a brief and unsuccessful episode in Czechoslovak politics.

[29] Cf. Kiesing, *Archiv der Gegenwart,* vol. 1 (1946), p. 1542; *Facts-on-File* (New York, 1946), p. 174.

[30] Cf. Hubert Ripka, *Czechoslovakia Enslaved* (London: Gollancz, 1950).

2: THE ENTRY OF CZECHOSLOVAKIA INTO THE COMMUNIST PARTY-STATE SYSTEM

The Communist Party of Czechoslovakia did not espouse the "bridge" concept, but its adoption by the noncommunist coalition members fitted well into the Party's strategy of the bid for absolute control. With good relationship to the Soviet Union as sacrosanct, the "bridge" image of Czechoslovakia helped to neutralize the resistance of the noncommunist elements; since it was difficult to dissociate communism and the U.S.S.R., a consistent and thorough criticism of the CPCS and its program and practices appeared impossible for fear of antagonizing the Kremlin.

The communists were determined to seize all power as soon as an opportunity would present itself. It seems, however, that they had no detailed plan for this purpose, and even less a firmly established timetable. Many contemporary sources and some later analyses by communist scholars tend to confirm the surmise that the CPCS alone—discounting foreign influence—had taken into consideration all eventualities, including that of a prolonged cooperation with non-communist parties in a coalition government, which would be confirmed in office by regularly held elections, on the 1946 pattern.[1] We can say with certainty that this lat-

[1] Cf. Klement Gottwald, *Collected Works*, vol. XII, p. 21; cf. also Zdeněk Mlynář, "Minulost a budoucnost naší státnosti"

31

ter possibility and line of action had been envisaged by a not negligible number of functionaries in the Party leadership.

The Coup d'État of February, 1948

The actual seizure of power by the CPCS in 1948 was prompted by several factors, among which the drive to revolution inherent to all communist parties was only one and not even the most important element. The reason why the "bridge" experiment came to an end relatively soon (though the "co-existence" between the communists and the noncommunists lasted longer in Czechoslovakia than in any other country in Central and Eastern Europe) lay, first of all, in the international situation of the late forties. By 1947, the Cold War had reached its first culmination point with several communist attempts to widen the area under their control (the civil war in Greece, nation-wide strikes in France and Italy) and with the first co-ordinated Western countermoves (Truman doctrine, Marshall Plan). The conflict between the Soviet Union and the Western Powers over Berlin was imminent.[2] Despite the foundation of the Cominform in September, 1947, the cohesion of the Soviet Bloc left much to be desired, and the split with Yugoslavia must then have appeared inevitable to all informed circles. Under these conditions, a substantial strengthening of the Soviet position in Central and Eastern Europe was considered necessary by the Kremlin policy makers. The

---

(The Past and the Future of Our State Institutions), *Právník* (Prague), May 1965, No. 5, pp. 397–412.

[2] Cf. E. McInnis, R. Hiscocks, R. Spencer, *The Shaping of Post-War Germany* (London: J. M. Dent, 1960), pp. 111–17.

Czechoslovak communists held the key to this important operation.

For the Communist Party of Czechoslovakia, its membership in the Cominform was of particular significance. The Party had been integrated into the communist system long before the whole state was absorbed into it. As the Czechoslovak CP was the strongest government party, the Cominform instructions to it were much more binding and meaningful than, for example, they would have been for another party of comparable size but remaining in opposition. The opportunity for independent maneuvering, provided the CPCS would have really wished for it, was thus further limited.

It seems, however, that the Party toed the new, tougher line willingly. On New Year's Eve, 1947, the Central Committee of the CPCS made public its intention to seek absolute majority at the next general election, slated for May, 1948.[3] Taken at face value, this declaration of intentions might still have been viewed as a pledge to observe the constitutional rules; on the other hand, the drive for undisputed control was unmistakable. In January, 1948, a communist Member of Parliament, Mr. Vodička, disclosed at a Party meeting that "the switches had been thrown over to the left," in both domestic and foreign politics.[4] As

[3] Cf. *Rudé právo* (Prague), December 31, 1947.

[4] The statement about "the switches thrown over to the left" was made by the Deputy Jan Vodička, Chairman of the Union of Anti-Fascist Combatants, at the Communist Party caucus at the Provincial National Committee of Bohemia, in Prague, January 15, 1948. In the first days of February, 1948, the CPCS presented a new list of "leftist" demands (further nationalizations, extension of the land reform, etc.) which were realized following the coup d'état. Cf. Pavel Reiman, *History of the CPCS*, p. 526.

the outcome of the next election was uncertain—it was virtually sure that the number of communist votes would not increase to the desired absolute majority; on the contrary, the polls of public opinion suggested that the Party would lose some of the electoral support obtained in 1946—the only course that remained open was the overthrow of the democratic order and the elimination of the uncomfortable coalition partners by force under one pretext or another.

The leaders of the noncommunist majority themselves soon provided such a pretext. After a disagreement with the communist members during a Cabinet session over the measures taken by the communist-controlled Ministry of Interior, all noncommunist Ministers resigned their posts on February 20, 1948. They expected that this move would either compel their communist colleagues to retreat in the disputed case or else render the government incapable of ruling and bring about its reconstruction by forcing premature elections. They counted on the full support of the President of the Republic, though later descriptions of the February events by direct participants suggest that there had been no, or at least not any sufficient, preliminary arrangements to that effect between the noncommunist politicians and the head of the State.[5]

The communists reacted in way quite unexpected by the noncommunist parties. The day following the resignation of the Cabinet Ministers, the Minister of Information, Václav Kopecký, a member of the CPCS politbureau, seized the control of all the Czechoslovak broadcasting facilities and put them at the service of

[5] Cf. Josef Laušmann: *Kdo byl vinen?* ("Who Was Guilty?") (Vienna: "Vorwärts" Printing Office, 1953), pp. 155–57; cf. also series of articles by Vladimír Krajina in the Czech exile monthly *Svobodný zítřek* (Paris), February-March-April, 1949.

the Communist Party, which thus gained tremendous advantage in publicizing its own version of the governmental crisis. The communists made every effort to present the cabinet crisis as a "treason of the highest national interests" and as an "act of sabotage against the Two-Year Economic Plan."[6] A public meeting was called by the Party Secretariat in the Old Town Square in Prague, where several thousand carefully hand-picked communists and fellow-travelers heard and approved the communist proposal for the solution of the crisis. While the President of the Republic tried to preserve the constitutional rule and to induce the communists to start talks with the representatives of the coalition parties toward the reconstruction of the government, the Communist Party, in control of the Ministry of Interior and consequently of the police, prevented further activity of all noncommunist organizations by sealing off their premises, closing down the editorial offices of their newspapers, and by sporadic arrests of their leading members. Finally, on February 25, 1948, under the threat of a general strike called by the communist-controlled Trade Unions, the President of the Republic, Eduard Beneš, approved the Cabinet list sponsored by the Communist Party. This new government, the "government of the Renewed National Front," gave the communists the desired absolute majority: Not only was the number of Cabinet posts assigned to communists increased, regardless of the proportion of polled votes and Parliament seats, but several ministries were also turned over to the representatives of the Revolutionary Trade Unions, Youth Movement, National Peasant Union, the National Council of Women, etc. These so-called mass-organi-

[6] Cf. Pavel Reiman, *History of the CPCS*, pp. 531–32.

zations were, in reality, either agencies of the Communist Party, communist front organizations, or in hands of communist symapthizers and fellow-travelers.

In order to assure the control of the Parliament, the new government deprived a large number of noncommunist deputies of their mandates, on the grounds that they had committed high treason. Purges were carried out in all organs of the local government in provinces and districts as well as in the administrative apparatus. The "enemies of the people's democratic order" were expelled from schools and scientific institutions, from the press, and from radio, cinema and theater. These purges were conducted by special Action Committees, mostly self-elected bodies composed of "progressive elements" among the staff of each office and institution.

The Transformation of Czechoslovakia into a Communist Party State

One of the first acts of the government of the Renewed National Front was to embark upon a new stage of nationalization. The Presidential Decree of October, 1945, implementing the Košice Program, had left the majority of industrial enterprises with 500 and fewer employees in private hands; the post-February wave of nationalization not only brought every plant with 50 or more workers under state control, but also many smaller enterprises and workshops were expropriated if they fell under the category of "vitally important" industries or trades. A congress of the communist-sponsored United National Peasant Organization which took place immediately after the February crisis laid the foundations for the later collectivization of agriculture.[7]

[7] *Ibid.*, p. 529 and p. 550.

It was in this climate that general elections were scheduled for May, 1948. There was no reason to expect that the election would change anything substantial in the new order of things. Only a single list of candidates was permitted, with a blank ballot as the sole alternative for those who did not want to support the renewed National Front." However, the decision to hold the May, 1948, election on the pattern of a plebiscite, with one list only, had not been taken immediately after the coup d'état. It had been understood, at first, that all political parties, "cleansed" of anti-communist elements, would go to the polls separately. The Czechoslovak information media, during the first six weeks after the February crisis, often suggested this possibility. It was only in April that the Revolutionary Trade Union Movement, or rather its Chairman, member of the Communist Party Politburo and the Vice-Premier Antonín Zápotocký, presented the demand "of all working people of Czechoslovakia" to admit only "a joint ballot of all progressive elements of the National Front."[8] It is possible that the opinion on this question was then divided among the Party leadership. There has been lately more evidence to substantiate this surmise.[9]

The National Assembly which issued from this election claimed a popular support comparable to that recorded in other people's democracies, though this alleged support had not yet reached the nearly 100 percent level of the late fifties. The voice of the opposition was still clearly preceptible. According to the figures published by the authorities, 86.6 percent of votes were cast in favor of the National Front. The seats in the National Assembly and in the government

[8] Cf. *Rudé právo* (Prague), April 8, 1948.
[9] Cf. Zdeněk Mlynář, *Právník*, pp. 397–412.

were so divided among the different parties and mass organizations as to give the communists a safe majority of two-thirds. The same predetermined formula has been applied ever since to all elections which have taken place after 1948.[10]

Following the pre-February agreements between the coalition partners, the main task of the Parliament elected in May was to give Czechoslovakia a new constitution.[11] This document, the Constitution of May 9, which was an official anniversary of the liberation of Czechoslovakia by the Red Army, still bore some characteristics of a Western-type democracy although it had been adopted by the already Renewed National Front. Neither formal sanctions of the administrative practices introduced after the coup d'état nor explicit confirmation of the privileged position of the Communist Party were contained anywhere in the text. On the other hand, it was not a purely liberal constitution any more. President Eduard Beneš refused to sign it because he found specific clauses "undemocratic." Unable to make the National Assembly accept his views, he resigned on June 7, 1948, and was succeeded by the former Prime Minister Gottwald, Chairman of the Communist Party. With the departure of Mr. Beneš, the last prominent noncommunist personality and the last advocate of the "bridge" concept disappeared from the political scene. The process of Czechoslovakia's transformation into a communist party state was thus completed.

[10] Elections to the Parliament took place in November, 1954 (97.89 percent of votes for the National Front ballot), and in June, 1960 (99.76 percent for the National Front).

[11] Cf. *Ústava 9. května* ("The Constitution of 9th May") (Prague: Orbis, 1951); cf. also Pavel Reiman, *History of the CPCS*, p. 538.

3: INTENSIVE SOCIALIST DEVELOPMENT OF CZECHOSLOVAKIA

The entry of Czechoslovakia into the communist party-state system did not in itself bring any nearer the remedy for the "integrational dichotomy" from which the country had been suffering. Under the new conditions, this traditional contradiction just took different forms; the political center of gravity had been transferred from the West to the East, but the new orientation was less than ever before in agreement with the "natural" integration trends in the Central European area. The government of communist Czechoslovakia displayed its greatest dependence upon the Soviet center of power at that time, and made serious and systematic efforts to bring the two elements into harmony by adjusting the economy through shifts similar to those previously effected on the political level. However, since the basic facts of economy cannot be changed on command and even less so in a short span of time, the problems which the Czechoslovak party state inherited from the pre-communist era not only remained unresolved but became accentuated.

Assimilation and Uniformization

In the late forties and in the early fifties, Czechoslovakia made rapid progress toward uniformity with

39

other communist party states. Although the Constitution of May 9 had explicitly guaranteed the private ownership of enterprises with fifty or fewer employees, the nationalization of industry continued apace, so that by 1950 almost all means of production were incorporated in the socialist sector. At the same time, all trades, including small retail businesses, were taken over by the state. Service enterprises—repair shops, hairdressers, laundries, restaurants, etc.—passed without exception into the ownership of communal authorities.[1] Only the agricultural sector remained, for a considerable length of time, mainly under private ownership. By the time when the majority of communist party states appeared to have concluded the era of intensive socialist development, i.e., by the end of the Stalinist period, less than half of the arable land in Czechoslovakia was collectivized.[2]

In the process of adjusting Czechoslovakia's economy to the Soviet model, the overall design of Czechoslovak industrial structure was thoroughly transformed. The pre-communist Czechoslovakia had been an economically developed country, with production focused on both heavy and light industry. The post-1948 application of the Soviet blueprint for "socialism in one country" to Czechoslovak conditions stressed development of heavy industry.

The first Five-Year Plan, launched on January 1, 1949, provided for an average expansion of industrial production by 57 percent. The base for comparison

[1] *Czechoslovakia: An Area Manual* (Chevy Chase, Md.: Operations Research Office, The Johns Hopkins University, 1955), vol. II (June), pp. 277–81.
[2] In 1956, only 27.6 percent of arable land was under cultivation by Uniform Agricultural Cooperatives; cf. *Mechanisace zemědělstvi* May 6, 1956.

was the level attained in 1948, which equaled roughly the industrial output in 1937. However, the targets for metallurgy and heavy machinery were increased by 93 percent and 100 percent respectively. In February, 1951, the original goals were revised and the planned output in heavy industry was raised by approximately 80 percent. Out of a total of 482,000 new workers expected to take jobs during the Five-Year Plan, 170,000—more than one third—were directed into heavy industry. Two subsequent Five-Year Plans (1954–1958, and 1959–1963, scrapped in 1961) were drawn along the same lines, giving an absolute priority to the development of heavy industrial potential.[3] By the use of methods suitable for underdeveloped countries which strive at a rapid equalization of their economic levels with those of advanced nations, the Czechoslovak economy was thrown out of balance, and the adverse effects of this shift have not been overcome to the present day.

As in the neighboring communist party states, the Party gradually extended its control over all spheres of public life. A thorough reform of the school system was put into effect in 1948; Marxist philosophy and communist ideology became compulsory subjects in all higher grades, and the entire teaching staff underwent intensive indoctrination. Religious instruction was discouraged and limited by special administrative measures. The churches were subjected to strong pressure, even to persecution, especially after a conflict arose between the State and the Catholic bishops, in 1949, over a pastoral letter stressing the incompatibility of Marxist materialism and Christian religion.[4] In 1951, all

[3] For more detailed information, see Paul Thad-Alton, *Czechoslovak National Income and Product 1947/48 and 1955/56* (New York: Columbia University Press, 1962).

[4] Mario Hikl, *The Penal Codes in Communist Czechoslovakia,*

voluntary recreational and social organizations, regardless of their purpose, were either dissolved or subordinated to a new body called "Svazarm," which was a nation-wide union for pre- and paramilitary training. Various clubs and associations of scientists, journalists, writers, and artists were focused into nation-wide organizations, one for each profession, under the direct supervision of Party officials. Publishing of newspapers, periodicals, and books was made subject to censorship, the efficacy of which was substantially increased by the prevailing system of paper rationing. Stage productions became closely guarded. The film industry had been nationalized as early as in 1945 and fell now under the jurisdiction of the Ministry of Culture, as did radio and television networks, which had operated with state participation or under state control since their foundation. In carrying out these measures of reorganization, the Party also followed, in most cases, the Soviet model.

The entire military organization was put under a direct Party control. The officer corps was purged of all "unreliable" elements and those who were purged, down to the lowest echelons, were replaced by candidates with communist background or of working-class origin. The Soviet pattern was imitated to the minutest detail: military ranks and distinctions were taken over, Soviet uniforms copied, and political indoctrination introduced as one of the Army's principal tasks.

(Toronto: Czechoslovak Foreign Institute in Exile, 1957). See later admissions by Czechoslovak jurists, concerning "excesses of the personality cult in the judiciary," such as: Vojtěch Hatala, "Kult osobnosti a niektoré noetické a etické problémy nášho trestného práva" ("The Personality Cult and some Noetical and Ethical Problems of Our Criminal Law"), *Právny obzor* (Bratislava) No. 2 (1964); and the minutes of the Scientific Conference on the Guarantees of Socialist Legality held in Smolenice, in Slovakia, from Nov. 21 to Nov. 23, 1963.

The police and the judiciary became instruments of the regime in its strive for the consolidation of absolute power. Despite explicit guarantees contained in the Constitution of 1948, the repressive apparatus was given free hand in dealing with political offenses. The organs of the State Security (political police) could arrest citizens without warrant and hold them for an indefinite period of time without trial and even without the assistance of a legal counsel. Moreover, the preliminary investigation was conducted by the office of the public prosecutor so that the court, during the actual trial, had to depend exclusively on data collected by the prosecution. The principle of presumption of innocence was reversed: the defendant was considered guilty unless he himself could prove the contrary. A sole confession by the accused, made during the first interrogation or at the time of the trial, was accepted as sufficient evidence and ground for his conviction [5] This Inquisition-like legal procedure was further aggravated through constant interference by Party officials who instructed the judges on the handling of individual cases. Czechoslovak justice became like justice in all other party states and according to the official thesis, "a weapon in the class struggle."[6]

Police terror wielded against real or potential opponents of the Party started as early as February, 1948, and reached its peak in about 1950 with several mass trials for crimes qualified as "conspiracy against the people's democratic order" or "high treason."[7] Often

[5] *Ibid.*
[6] *Ibid.*
[7] One of the most infamous trials of this series was staged in June 1950, when Mrs. Milada Horáková, member of parliament and an anti-Nazi resistance leader, was sentenced to death. At later trials, the whole leadership of the Social Democratic

43

the indictment was merely a pretext to seize the property of the defendant or to get rid of a difficult person against whom no other repressive measure had been found suitable by the regime. A special law on the establishment of forced labor camps (TNP), passed as early as 1948, provided another means of liquidating political adversaries. This legislation gave organs of the local government, the National Committees, the right to confine to a forced labor camp any person deemed hostile or dangerous to the established order, for a period up to two years, without any previous or subsequent legal action.[8] The practice of "putting justice at the service of the Socialist revolution" continued all through the fifties and was widely used during the collectivization campaign against the "kulaks," in order to intimidate possible opposition against the creation of Uniform Agricultural Cooperatives (JZD). Stiff sentences were the rule after capital punishment gradually became rarer.[9]

Living conditions were soon felt to be intolerable by many citizens, who often chose to escape to the West as the only means of self-preservation. During the first

---

Party was handed stiff jail sentences; former communists were tried, too, as "trotskyist saboteurs."

[8] Cf. Law No. 247, Oct. 25, 1948, in *Sbírka zákonů Československé republiky* ("Collected Laws of the Czechoslovak Republic"), 1948, pp. 1530–31. The power to send recalcitrant citizens of the people's democratic state to labor camps did not, however, rest long with the National Committees. Law No. 87 of July 12, 1950, transferred this prerogative to the courts. Finally, the new Penal Code of December 1956 does not list labor camps any more among the penal institutions of Czechoslovakia. (Cf. Law No. 64, Dec. 19, 1956, "Collected Laws of the Czechoslovak Republic," 1956, pp. 199–266).

[9] Ladislav Feierabend, *Agricultural Cooperatives in Czechoslovakia* (Washington: Mid-European Study Center, 1952), pp. 67–69.

three years of communist rule, about 70,000 Czechs and Slovaks left the country illegally or remained abroad in those rare instances when they succeeded in obtaining a passport.[10] The regime took countermeasures in order to prevent further flights. An "Iron Curtain" was established along the western borders of Czechoslovakia officially to protect the country "from the infiltration of foreign agents and spies." It was a solid structure of electricity-charged barbed wire, ditches, mine fields, and machine-gun towers, constructed on the Soviet pattern and guarded by special army detachments. The Czechoslovak Iron Curtain completed the network of similar installations along the western frontiers of European communist party states, as a tangible symbol of the incorporation of Czechoslovakia into the communist system.

The CPCS during the Stalinist Period

Although only one joint ballot of all member organizations of the National Front was admitted in each election held after February, 1948, the noncommunist political parties remained formally independent, kept secretariats and staffs of their own, and held members' meetings and conferences regularly. From this point of view, the Czechoslovak party state differed from most other communist party states, especially from the Soviet model.[11] The only simplification of the existing parties

[10] Louise W. Holborne, *The International Refugee Organization—A Specialized Agency of the United Nations* (London: Oxford University Press, 1956), p. 182.

[11] Formally independent political parties exist, at present, only in Bulgaria, Czechoslovakia, East Germany and Poland. Cf. Lucienne Rey and Zdenek Suda, "Les partis politiques noncommunistes en Europe Centrale et Orientale," *Est-&-Ouest* (Paris), July 1963, no. 303.

spectrum was the merger, in June 1948, of the Social Democratic Party with the CPCS. The merger was carried out as an action of individuals, with each member of the Socialist Party joining the CPCS "voluntarily," on the basis of a separate application for membership. The success of this campaign was a foregone conclusion since there was no alternative; the former Social Democrats could only become communists or stand apart and be singled out as "negative elements," because the Socialist Party had to disappear under any circumstances.

After the merger, the CPCS availed itself of the twenty-three parliament seats which previously had been held by the Social Democrats and its ranks increased by some 500,000 members. However, the most significant influx of fresh adherents after the coup d'état came from strata other than Socialist. Many Party sympathizers, as yet not organized, and a sizable proportion of the membership of the remaining four noncommunist parties joined the CPCS in the first months after February and brought the total to approximately 2,500,000. In comparison to the figures recorded before the first general election in May, 1946, the increase was equal to 150 percent. The CPCS became the strongest ruling party outside the Soviet Union and surpassed, in absolute terms, the size of the All-Union Communist Party of the Bolsheviks before 1945.[12]

The sudden and unprecedented growth of the Party ranks presented also certain risks. There was no doubt that a great portion of the postwar membership, espe-

[12] Until 1945, the All-Union Communist Party (of the Bolsheviks) had 2,477,666 registered members. It was only after the World War II that the ranks of the Party swelled to 5,760,000. Cf. J. M. Bocheński, *Handbuch des Weltkommunismus* (Freiburg: Karl Alber, 1958), p. 113.

cially that which joined the movement after the coup d'état, consisted either of opportunists or of persons who did not act upon their own free will, like the former Social Democrats. The iron discipline required by the communist principle of "democratic centralism" was thus exposed to a less than welcome "softening" influence. A substantial reduction of the Party membership appeared necessary. In a series of purges, officially presented as "verifications of membership cards," the total number was reduced to about one and a half million by 1951.[13]

These purges aimed, in principle, at the elimination of potentially dangerous components of the Communist Party. Despite the number of members involved, the consequences were by no means as dramatic and far-reaching as those of the purges employed by the leadership in the faction struggle, to dispose of dissident elements among Party cadres. Since the early fifties, the repressive apparatus of the State had been used, to an ever-increasing extent, in these intra-party disputes. Purges accompanied by show trials, frequent in the months preceding Stalin's death, continued until 1954. Some were undoubtedly sponsored by Moscow, to deter the more independent-thinking among the Party elites from eventually adopting the example of Tito's Yugoslavia; others seemed to be more homespun, prompted by controversies among leading Czechoslovak communists.

The most famous show-trial of the Stalinist period was that of the Party Secretary-General, Rudolf Slánský, and thirteen other prominent communist personalities, in November and December, 1952. It was officially

---

[13] Cf. Pavel Reiman, *History of the CPCS*, pp. 594–95; cf. also *Czechoslovakia: An Area Manual*, pp. 273–74.

labeled as the trial "of the anti-State conspiracy of Rudolf Slánský and his consorts." Eleven defendants were condemned to death and executed, among them also the former Minister of Foreign Affairs, a prominent Slovak communist Vlado Clementis. The Slánský trial had strong anti-Semitic flavor, in line with the purges organized in the Soviet Union towards the close of Stalin's lifetime.[14] To the extent to which the series of purges and of political processes assured uniformity of development with the other party states, they can be considered instruments of Stalinist "integration."

The liquidation of Rudolf Slánský started a movement which deeply affected the highest ranks of the Party. The most frequent targets of the persecution were those communists who had had some international background: former Comintern officials, communist leaders who had spent the Second World War in the West, members of the International Brigade in Spain during the Civil War 1936/38, and Jews.[15] The sentencing of Vlado Clementis appeared to be, most probably, Stalin's own way of settling an old disagreement with Clementis, who, as an exile in Paris in August, 1939, had denounced openly the Soviet-German Treaty. This trial also became a prelude to a wholesale campaign against the Slovak "bourgeois

[14] *Proces s vedením protistátního spikleneckého centra v čele s Rudolfem Slánským* ("Trial of the Anti-State Conspiratorial Center led by Rudolf Slánský"), published by the Czechoslovak Ministry of Justice, Prague 1953, p. 9.

[15] Sdělení Ústředního výboru KSČ o porušování stranických zásad a socialistické zákonnosti v období kultu osobnosti ("Report of the Central Committee of the CPCS on the Violation of the Party Principles and of Socialist Legality during the Period of the Cult of Personality"), presented at the Central Committee meeting, April 3–4, 1963, in Prague, and reprinted in the Czech exile magazine *Svědectví* VII/28 (spring 1966), pp. 350–84.

nationalists," a purge for which Stalin alone can hardly be made responsible; it continued long after his death and the main trial took place in Bratislava as late as in April, 1954.[16] The action against "bourgeois nationalism" reflected rather the difficulties which the Party had to face in the matter of integration within the nation, resulting from the unsolved problem of relations between the Czechs and the Slovaks. Since the February coup d'état, the strengthening of centralist tendencies in the Party leadership and the gradual reduction of the autonomous status of the Slovak communist organization had seriously aggravated the political climate in Slovakia; however, suppressing by force the overt signs of discontent did not bring any nearer a satisfactory solution of the problem.

The lingering survival of Stalinist methods was characteristic of the Czechoslovak situation in general; but the continuation of purges beyond the date of Stalin's death was also a part of strategy of the new Party leadership which took over after the execution of Rudolf Slánský and the sudden death of the Chairman Klement Gottwald (in March, 1953). This new team was almost exclusively composed of former officials of the Party apparatus. The Secretariat passed into the hands of Antonín Novotný, formerly in charge of the regional CP organization in the Prague region. For the rest, the majority of all important Party posts vacated by the purges before and after Stalin's death were occupied by younger people, previously functionaries of local organizations, close to Antonín Novotný. These cadres had a completely different background from that of their predecessors, who had been members of the Old Guard, tested in the political struggle

[16] *Ibid.*, p. 372; cf. also pp. 388–89.

during the first years of the Czechoslovak Communist movement.

The changes in Party leadership were accompanied by a thorough modification of the organizational set-up. There was no successor to the Party chief Klement Gottwald, as the function of the Chairman was abolished. Instead, a new organ, the Party Presidium, was introduced, which replaced also the Politburo, hitherto the policy-making body. The title of the Secretary General was changed into that of First Secretary, assisted by four Secretaries, each of whom was assigned a special responsibility in the Secretariat and in the Central Committee. Regional and district Party groups were recast along the same lines. The traditional organizational pattern carried over from the time of the First Republic, which had made the CPCS resemble other Czechoslovak political parties, thus gave way to a new structure, an almost perfect copy of the framework of the Communist party of the Soviet Union. During the period of intensive socialist development, the process of molding the Czechoslovak party state to make it resemble closely the Soviet model was accomplished also in the Party organization.

Vertical Integration

The progress of assimilation, however, did not automatically help to integrate Czechoslovakia into the communist party-state system. Similarity—or even uniformity—does not necessarily foster compatibility, the basic condition for integration. Uniformity by itself is rather a neutral element in integrative relationships. The factors determining the trends toward integration are the interests and the goals of the different social and political units involved in the integrative process. The common goals of two states having entirely unlike political or economic systems, for example, act as powerful agents of integration. Conversely, the divergent or opposed interests of two nations governed by similar or even identical systems lead necessarily to a conflict.[17]

The idea of integration had been unknown to Marxist theoreticians; even the term itself was proscribed among them for a long period of time.[18] Between the wars, the leaders of the communist parties in Central and Eastern Europe had envisaged that, upon a communist seizure of power, their countries would join the U.S.S.R. as additional republics of the Union in some form.[19]

It was, therefore, only logical that the political relations between the Soviet Union and the smaller European party states, after their entry into the communist system, became those of unreserved submission to the Soviet power center. In the economic sphere, this sub-

---

[17] In the case of totalitarian states, this argument can be pressed still further: The identity of political systems and ideologies implies opposition of interests and is, in itself, conflict-generating. The Reason of State ("die Staatsräson") in a totalitarian country claims absolute infallibility and is, consequently, absolutely intolerant. This intolerance is shown equally toward social and political units based on a different ideology, as toward organisms administered by the same political system. Every totalitarian state presumes to be the only orthodox interpreter of ideological dogmas. Therefore, it may be affirmed that uniformity of systems among totalitarian states is a factor opposing integration.

[18] Cf. V. I. Lenin, *Collected Works* (German Edition) (Moscow: Marx-Engels-Lenin Institute, 1956), vol. VI, p. 18, cf. English edition (1947), vol. II, pp. 175–77.

[19] Cf. Ferdinand Peroutka, *Budování státu* ("The Building of a State") (Prague: František Borový, 1931), vol. 4, pp. 2210–11.

mission was translated into a direct exploitation of the economies of the people's democracies by the Soviet Union. The links within the system were, on the whole, centripetally bilateral: The smaller party states were closely associated to the Soviet center of power and Soviet economy, but their mutual—"horizontal"—bonds remained very loose, almost nonexistent. This kind of integration, often called "vertical," was characteristic of the mutual relations between the U.S.S.R. and the communist countries in Central and Eastern Europe all through the Stalinist era, but it has prevailed, to a large extent, until the present time. The contemporary "polycentrist" tendencies, with all their spectacular manifestations, can be defined as a movement aiming at the reversal of the vertical trend.

The vertical integrative relationship between Czechoslovakia and the Soviet Union found its formal expression on the political level partly in the Soviet-Czechoslovak alliance (based on the Friendship and Mutual Assistance Treaty) and partly in the membership of the CPCS in the Cominform.[20] In addition to these two platforms, the Soviet Union could use the channels of direct inter-party contacts to assure coordination of Soviet and Czechoslovak policies. Through the Communist Party of Czechoslovakia, the Soviet leadership could also influence Czechoslovak domestic politics, sometimes determining the most minute details. Its influence was further increased by the extraordinary willingness of the Czechoslovak communists to follow the Soviet example in literally everything. The imitation of all that was Soviet was often pushed to the absurd.[21]

[20] See Chapter 1, "The Pre-Entry Period."
[21] In early fifties, for example, abacuses were introduced in banks, insurance businesses, and bureaus of statistics although

The Soviet and Czechoslovak foreign policy lines remained uniform during the entire period of intensive Socialist development. Czechoslovak diplomatic actions were always carefully co-ordinated with those of the Soviet Union, and Czechoslovak representatives in the United Nations and other international bodies invariably took identical stands on various world problems with the representatives of the U.S.S.R.[22] This close co-ordination existed not only in relation to states outside the communist sphere but also to other member countries of the communist system. The most typical example of the latter was the Soviet-Czechoslovak alignment toward Yugoslavia, after the Soviet-Yugoslav split in the summer of 1948. The Czechoslovak communist regime carried out the boycott directives of the Cominform to such an extent that its action was outstanding even among the other Cominform member countries.[23]

---

these organizations had been using, for many years, the most modern counting machines. This "improvement" was officially explained as an application of the Soviet model; in the Soviet Union, as in all underdeveloped countries, the abacus has been the common counting aid in current use.

[22] The Czechoslovak delegation in the United Nations, for example, supported all Soviet moves during the Korean war 1950–53, including the Soviet charge that the UN troops used bacteriological weapons. Czechoslovak delegates in the International Labor Organization opposed the discussion on labor camps in communist countries and boycotted the meetings when the talks took place. Czechoslovakia also suspended all cooperation with the International Refugee Organization and closed its Prague office although, officially, it had been one of its founding members. All these moves followed Soviet orders. The coordination of Soviet and Czechoslovak foreign policies had started before the coup d'état of 1948, but it was only in the fifties that the Czechoslovak Ministry of Foreign Affairs was given direct instructions from the Kremlin. Cf. James F. Byrnes, *Speaking Frankly* (New York: Harper and Brothers, 1947), pp. 143–44.

[23] Cf. *White Book on Aggressive Activities of the Governments*

53

There had been no formal integrative links between the Soviet and the Czechoslovak military organizations during Stalin's lifetime, as the Warsaw Treaty was not concluded until 1955. The absence of such bonds, however, did not constitute any obstacle to direct Soviet influence on Czechoslovak military policies and strategic planning. The Czechoslovak General Staff had to follow the instructions of special Red Army advisers. Although Czechoslovakia had always been an important arms-manufacturing country, standard Soviet weapons were gradually introduced in all army units, which further strengthened the military dependence of Czechoslovakia on the Soviet Union. Soviet experts also helped to set up Czechoslovak police forces, especially those charged with the repression of political offenses (State Security, Border Guards). The entire police organization, following the Soviet model, was put on a military basis. During the great purges and show trials in 1951–1953, the investigation was often conducted under the supervision of Soviet police officials.[24]

The bilateral links joining Czechoslovakia to the Soviet Union were particularly strong in the economic sphere. These links, because they were established between the dominating power center and one of the dominated subcenters, have already been classified as "centripetally bilateral" or "vertical," as opposed to "peripherally bilateral" or "horizontal" links which

---

of the USSR, Poland, Czechoslovakia, Hungary, Rumania, Bulgaria and Albania towards Yugoslavia (Belgrade: Ministry of Foreign Affairs of the Federal People's Republic of Yugoslavia, 1951), pp. 146–53, 139, 219–21, 243–45, 302–3, 448, 476–77.

[24] Cf. Vlastimil Chalupa, *Rise and Development of A Totalitarian State* (Leiden: H. E. Stenfert Kroese N.V., 1959), pp. 223, 243, and 244.

exist between two dominated party states. In the case of Czechoslovakia, a part of the centripetal linkage was developed on the basis that had been laid during the pre-entry period. As early as in December, 1947, a special treaty on scientific, technical and economic cooperation was signed between the two countries. Prior to that, the Soviet Union, in pursuance of agreements reached with the Allied governments during World War II, took control of several Czechoslovak key industrial enterprises, such as the uranium mines in Jáchymov and the large synthetic-gasoline plant in Záluží near Most. Even though later the ownership of these industries was returned to Czechoslovak authorities, the U.S.S.R. usually reserved for itself extensive privileges and priority purchase rights. As a consequence, large quantities of important industrial products and rare raw materials were exported from Czechoslovakia to the Soviet Union. On the other hand, substantial deliveries of Soviet raw materials and food to Czechoslovakia (especially of wheat, which began in the drought year of 1947, allegedly as a compensation for Czechoslovakia's withdrawal from the Marshall Plan) increased considerably the modest pre-war volume of Soviet-Czechoslovak economic exchange. If, in 1937, the Soviet Union participated by only one percent in the Czechoslovak foreign trade turnover, in 1947 its share already equaled 4.9 percent.[25]

However, after the communist coup d'état, Czechoslovak trade with the Soviet Union developed at an even faster pace. In 1950, it attained 169 percent of the value registered in 1948; in 1952, 254 percent; in

[25] Cf. *Statistický zpravodaj* ("The Statistical Bulletin"), (Prague: National Statistical Office, 1948), vol. IX, no. 9 (Sept. 1948), p. 337.

1954, 301 percent. In 1957, it represented no less than 31 percent of the country's total trade turnover, more than the sum of the exchanges with all "capitalist" countries, the trade with whom rapidly decreased at the same time.[26]

The special nature of the economic relations between Czechoslovakia and the Soviet Union was reflected also in the kind of products exchanged. Food and raw materials constituted more than three-fourths of the Soviet exports to Czechoslovakia. In 1958, the Soviet Union provided 99 percent of Czechoslovakia's aluminium, 98 percent of manganese ore, 90 percent of nickel, 85 percent of rubber, 75 percent of copper, 74 percent of iron ore, and 55 percent of cotton. It assured, furthermore, 90 percent of the Czechoslovak consumption of corn, 50 percent of wheat, and 50 percent of rye.[27] On the other hand, Czechoslovakia supplied 88 percent of the Soviet Union's automobile imports, 44 percent of its leather footwear imports, 32 percent of furniture imports, and 13 percent of ready-made clothes and linen imports. The U.S.S.R. was buying 99 percent of all Czechoslovak exports of capital goods in the sector of chemical industry, 90 percent of all exported ships, 84 percent of capital goods for iron works, foundries, and rolling mills, and 70 percent of the railway rolling stock reserved for export. In terms of the Czechoslovak trade turnover, Soviet deliveries represented 33 percent of all imported industrial raw materials and 44 percent of all imported food. Soviet purchases in Czechoslovakia equaled 35 percent of all Czechoslovak exports of capital goods and 43 percent of

[26] *Rovnost* (daily, Brno), Nov. 8, 1957.
[27] *Nová svoboda* (daily, Ostrava), Dec. 13, 1958; and *Zahraniční obchod* ("The Foreign Trade") (Prague), Nov. 1962, no. 11.

all exported commodities.[28] Measured by the volume of the Czechoslovak industrial production, these figures are even more impressive. In 1952, for example, Czechoslovakia exported to the U.S.S.R. 90 percent of its entire production of penicillin.

This intensification of mutual trade relations put Czechoslovakia in the second place among all trade partners of the Soviet Union. However, in order to assess correctly the consequences for both countries of this very close co-operation, we must consider the role which this exchange of goods played in the national economies of the U.S.S.R. and Czechoslovakia. The Soviet Union depends to a much lesser degree on foreign trade than the communist party states in Central and Eastern Europe. Exports represent but a fraction of the Soviet national product, a situation similar to that of the United States.[29] Czechoslovakia, on the other hand, has always exported a substantial part of its industrial production and imported great quantities of raw materials.[30] If we compare, in addition, the geographical size and the human potential of the U.S.S.R. with those of Czechoslovakia, we will readily understand that the fact of being the second foremost among the Soviet Union's trade counterparts must have meant much more to the Czechoslovak economy than to that of the Soviet Union. It is interesting to note that the only other party state which can match Czechoslo-

[28] Cf. *Rudé právo* (Prague), Nov. 22, 1962; *Technický týdeník* ("Technology Weekly"), Dec. 1962, no. 50; and *Radio Prague*, July 21, 1963.

[29] Cf. *Vneshniaia Torgovlia Soiuza SSR* ("Foreign Trade of the U.S.S.R.") (Moscow: Izdatelstvo Meshdunarodnie Otnoshenia, 1966), pp. 17 and 19.

[30] Cf. *The Statistical Yearbook 1934*, pp. 128–29; *Statistický zpravodaj* (Prague) vol. XI, no. 4, April 1948, p. 165; *The Statistical Yearbook 1966*, pp. 428–29.

vakia's level of economic development, namely East Germany, ranks first in the list of the trade partners of the U.S.S.R.[31]

Under these conditions, the vertical integrative relationship of the small, industrially mature country with the economically underdeveloped but politically and militarily powerful nation had to take the form of exploitation, especially since the latter was in the position to dictate to the former the terms of economic co-operation.

Soviet exploitation of Czechoslovak economy did not take place only in direct Soviet-Czechoslovak trade contacts. An effective instrument in this respect was the so-called "triangle trade" in which three countries were participating, usually the U.S.S.R. and two smaller communist party states. Since the Soviet government could determine not only the prices for which it purchased the goods from Czechoslovakia, but also the prices of the goods sold to Czechoslovakia, and since this arrangement prevailed in the economic contacts with all communist countries in Central and Eastern Europe, any business transaction involving the resale of merchandise bought by the U.S.S.R. from a smaller communist partner was highly advantageous to the Soviets. An example of this profitable re-export was the sale by the Soviet Union, in the early fifties, of tobacco purchased in Bulgaria for an imposed price extremely favorable to the buyer, to Czechoslovakia, who had to pay for these deliveries by supplying the U.S.S.R. with valuable industrial goods, again for prices dictated by Moscow, considerably under the world price level.[32]

[31] Cf. *Zahraniční obchod*, Nov. 1962, no. 11, pp. 3–6.
[32] Cf. *Czechoslovakia—An Area Manual*, vol. I (June 1955), pp. 37–38.

The triangle trade has not always been limited to the countries within the communist system. Often the Soviet authorities tried to apply this method in trading with Western states, in order to obtain goods for which their own economy could not offer equivalent products attractive enough to the seller country. For instance, in 1958, negotiations started between the U.S.S.R., Sweden, and Czechoslovakia, with the view of compensating Swedish deliveries of high quality iron ores to the Soviet Union by the export to Sweden of Czechoslovak chemicals, optical instruments, and crystal glass. This trade operation did not materialize, but it was understood that in the case of its realization the Soviets would pay Czechoslovakia in inconvertible roubles for the goods supplied to Sweden.[33]

It is probable that not all aspects of the economic policy pursued during the period of intensive socialist development met with a unanimous approval of the leaders of the Communist Party of Czechoslovakia. The centripetal integration trend, especially the almost exclusive binding of Czechoslovak economy to that of the Soviet Union, must have appeared to some elements among the communist cadres and élites as excessively onerous in terms of benefit-cost relationship. This opposition seems to have been crushed mainly during the great purges in the fifties. Though other charges leveled, for example, against the former Secretary General Rudolf Slánský and his co-defendants, in December, 1952, seem highly dubious, their indictment as having "sought a specific Czechoslovak way to socialism" and "worked toward increasing the dependence of Czechoslovakia on the economy of capitalist countries"

[33] Information Items, Radio Free Europe Archives, Munich, 1958.

may not have been altogether without substance.[34] It is perhaps not an accident, either, that the volume of Czechoslovak trade with non-communist countries reached its lowest point in the year immediately following the Slánský trial.[35]

First Attempts at Horizontal Integration

The vertical trend of integrative relationships which prevailed in Central and Eastern Europe during the Stalinist period obstructed seriously the development of multilateral and horizontal contacts among the smaller members of the system. Moreover, the Soviet power center was not only disinterested in fostering direct relations on the horizontal level, but rather suspicious of such relations: Politically, they threatened the monopoly of Soviet influence in the area; economically, they could divert the flow of goods from the centripetal channels and compete with relations profitable to the U.S.S.R., such as the "triangle" exchanges. The small communist party states themselves, in adopting the Soviet model of "socialism in one country,"

[34] Cf. *Proces s vedením protistátního spikleneckého centra v čele s Rudolfem Slánským* ("Trial against the Antistate Conspiratorial Center headed by Rudolf Slánský") (Prague: Ministerstvo spravedlnosti, 1953), pp. 77–78, 321–24, 356–58.

[35] Foreign trade with the so-called capitalist countries (the term includes also developing areas) from 1948 until 1965 shows the following figures: In 1948, 60.3 percent of the total volume; in 1949, 54.0 percent; in 1950, 44.4 percent; in 1951, 39.5 percent; in 1952, 28.6 percent; in 1953, 21.6 percent; in 1954, 25.2 percent; in 1955, 30.0 percent; in 1956, 34.2 percent; in 1957, 32.4 percent; in 1958, 29.5 percent; in 1959, 27.8 percent; in 1960, 28.5 percent; in 1961, 30.3 percent; in 1962, 25.8 percent; in 1963, 25.4 percent; in 1964, 26.7 percent; in 1965, 26.7 percent. Cf. Prokop Macháň, "Czechoslovak Foreign Trade," RFE Archives, Munich 1966.

strengthened autarchic tendencies in their national economies. A consistent application of the Soviet blueprint for industrial development resulted inevitably in reducing the part played by foreign trade in the national product and consumption patterns in people's democracies; and thus their interest in exchanges with the rest of the world, including other members of the communist system, diminished.

Political integration among the countries in Central and Eastern Europe made little peripheral progress in the years of intensive Socialist development, while the centripetal links to the Soviet Union were being strengthened. The leaderships, of all communist parties, remembering the violently negative Soviet reaction to the Yugoslav-Bulgarian initiative launched in early 1948 with a view of creating a Balkan federation, refrained from any similar venture.[36] Czechoslovakia was linked to many other party states by special bilateral friendship and cooperation treaties: to Poland, by a pact signed in 1947; to Bulgaria, by a treaty from 1948; to East Germany, by a special agreement on the inviolability of present borders, concluded in 1950. However, these treaties remained declarations of good will and nothing more, since it was only the alliance with the U.S.S.R. which really counted, and since all eventual co-operation with other party states had to be approved by the power center in Moscow. This state of affairs was reflected in the fact that, in the early fifties, traveling to the West, though difficult enough, was hampered by fewer obstacles than traveling to and from the communist countries.[37] Direct military ties

[36] Cf. Milovan Djilas, *Conversations with Stalin* (New York: Harcourt, Brace & World Inc., 1962), pp. 171–180.

[37] The Iron Curtain, for example, was first of all erected by the U.S.S.R. at the Czechoslovak-Soviet border in 1945; while

between Czechoslovakia and the communist party states other than the Soviet Union were, for all practical purposes, nonexistent.

Czechoslovakia's foreign economic relations, too, were almost exclusively of a vertical nature, with the U.S.S.R. as trade partner overshadowing all the other states of the system. Though the imports from and the exports to the Soviet Union increased about three times within the first five years after the seizure of power by the Communist Party, the trade with the smaller communist nations developed considerably slower. In most cases its ratio of growth remained the same as during the first post-war years; with some party states the volume of trade even decreased.[38]

Because of the economic policies imposed by the U.S.S.R. upon Czechoslovakia and all the other Communist Bloc countries, the first initiative aiming at economic integration on the horizontal level of the people's democracies, namely the creation of the Council of Mutual Economic Aid (COMECON) in 1949, could aim for but limited results. Czechoslovakia was one of the six founding members of this organization, together with Bulgaria, Hungary, Poland, Rumania,

---

in the fifties Czechoslovakia still had railroad and air connections to all West European capitals several times a day, the traffic to the U.S.S.R. and all the other people's democracies was much less frequent. In addition to the time necessary for the obtaining of a passport, a Czechoslovak citizen needed six months or more to secure a visitor visa to a "people's democracy." In 1952, Prague maintained its connection to the West by a railroad service including three express trains per day; railroad service to the communist countries operated, in some cases, only three times a week. Road communications with these states were as good as nonexistant. *Úřední jizdní řád ČSD* ("Czechoslovak official railroad guide") 1951/52.

[38] Cf. *The Statistical Yearbook 1958*, p. 316, particularly data concerning trade with Albania, Poland, and East Germany.

and the Soviet Union. East Germany became member in 1950; also Albania joined in 1950, but ceased to participate in the COMECON activities in 1961 after its break with the U.S.S.R.; Mongolia did not join until 1961, and Yugoslavia was not admitted until later, in 1965, as a signatory with limited rights and obligations. Though the officially indicated motive for the establishment of the COMECON was "the defense against economic discrimination of the Socialist states on the part of the imperialist powers," it was actually meant as a counterpart to the Organization of European Economic Cooperation which had originated from the European Recovery Program (Marshall Plan). The Council of Mutual Economic Aid, during the first years of its existence, was a strictly international organization, cautiously avoiding anything which might have suggested supranational ambitions.[39] It did not even possess, for a long time, any organs of its own, the only governing body being the irregularly called meetings of the Ministers of Economy of the member countries.

For reasons already cited, the economic contacts within the framework of the COMECON could never reach the intensity characteristic of Western international—let alone supranational—groupings. The nature of relations among the COMECON states is best illustrated by the fact that all through the period of intensive socialist development and even later on, the signatory nations conducted trade on an inelastic barter basis—goods for goods—and that the clearing points (surpluses

[39] Piotr Jaroszewicz, Polish Minister and Permanent Delegate in the COMECON, declared, Dec. 17, 1959: "The publication of the Charter of the Council of Mutual Economic Aid, deposited at the Organization of the United Nations, will put an end, once and for all, to all speculations about the allegedly supranational character of the COMECON." Cf. Radio Warsaw, December 17, 1959.

and deficits of the trade balance) had to be settled in hard currencies (U.S. dollars or Swiss Francs).[40] The COMECON remained, for many years, merely a loose platform for bilateral negotiations between the member governments and for theoretical discussions on co-operation projects which seldom were binding for the relevant parties. To the Soviet Union, on the other hand, it offered a practical advantage in providing a lever of command by which the Kremlin could influence and exploit the national economies of the smaller party states. In spite of its horizontal structure, the effect of the COMECON was rather vertical. Here, the same process of deformation could be observed as in the political sphere. Czechoslovakia's membership in the COMECON, under the impact of Stalinist policies, turned out to be but an economic variant of the Soviet-Czechoslovak alliance.

[40] Cf. Michael Kaser, *Comecon—Integration Problems of the Planned Economies* (London: Oxford University Press, 1965), p. 138.

4: THE POST-STALIN ERA

The period of intensive socialist development is not identical with the actual time of Stalin's rule, but some two or three years longer. This is true for all communist countries within the Soviet power orbit. All Western observers agree that the actual "de-Stalinization" or "thaw" did not set on in any party state before the Twentieth Congress of the Soviet Communist Party in February, 1956. In the case of Czechoslovakia, even this date would appear too early. Czechoslovak official sources sometimes claim that "the efforts to overcome the errors of the personality cult era" had started in Czechoslovakia in 1954,[1] but all available evidence contradicts this assertion. Not only did the methods of control current during Stalin's lifetime—purges and show trials—continue in 1954; even the "personality cult" in the narrowest sense of the word survived, for a long time, the death of the personality himself. It was only on May 1, 1955, that the huge Stalin Monument dominating the Prague panorama was unveiled. However, more important than the proliferation of the outward symbols of Stalinism was the persistence of the regime in "dogmatic" policies, which characterized the

[1] Cf. Pavel Reiman, *History of the CPCS*, p. 597.

post-Stalin, "pre-thaw" period in Czechoslovakia for several years, in contrast to more rapid development observed in other party states, particularly in Hungary and in Poland.

The Transitory Period

The death of Stalin and Gottwald did not change the general attitude of the CPCS and even less its allegiance to Moscow. The only sign of a more "independent" line of thought could be sensed in the fact that the Czechoslovak communists embarked upon the new paths traced by the CPSU with an even greater caution than Stalin's heirs in the Kremlin. Economic difficulties, which had become particularly serious in 1950 and which the regime's propaganda later attributed to "the traitor Rudolf Slánský and his gang," did not, of course, subside with the mere change in leadership. In order to counteract a very severe inflation and to raise the low morale of industrial workers, the successors of Gottwald had to carry out a drastic monetary reform in June, 1953, which practically wiped out the nation's savings. At the same time, the rationing of consumer goods, dating from the war, was abolished and prices of commodities were substantially raised. The hardships resulting from these measures stirred great unrest among the working population. In the main industrial centers—Plzeň, Kladno and Ostrava—workers went on strike. Demonstrations took place which the government could suppress only with the help of the army. This massive outbreak of discontent was the first in Central and Eastern Europe since the seizure of power by the communists and preceded by about two weeks the East Berlin uprising of June 17, 1953.[2]

In contrast with similar later events, such as the Poznan revolt in May, 1956, neither the riots in Czechoslovakia in June, 1953, nor the workers' rebellion in East Berlin initiated any "liberalization" trend in the European regions of the communist party-state system. The Communist Party of Czechoslovakia, despite the alarm signals, did not seem to possess enough courage to change the old course. It clung to it even more as serious difficulties manifested themselves in agriculture. The process of the "socialization of the countryside," i.e. collectivization, suffered heavy setbacks. In 1953 the collectivized sector of the farm production was still in clear minority and the Uniform Agricultural Cooperatives, which were set up to convince the private farmers of the advantages of collectivization, operated at great loss. Beginning with the summer of that year, many Agricultural Cooperatives were disbanded by the spontaneous decision of their members. The regime was left with no choice other than to legalize temporarily these dissolutions.[3]

The Tenth Congress of the Communist Party of Czechoslovakia, in June, 1954, did not put forward any new ideas or solutions. Conservatism appeared to the leadership to be the best policy. In the long run, this policy was not tenable, if for no other reason than because of the close links between Czechoslovakia and the power center in the U.S.S.R. The fact of being "vertically" integrated in the communist system, far

[2] Cf. *ibid.*, p. 584; cf. also William E. Griffith, *Communism in Europe*, vol. 2, p. 218.

[3] Cf. speech by President Antonín Zápotocký at the Klíčov dam, as reported by Radio Prague, August 1, 1953; cf. also Pavel Reiman, *History of the CPCS*, p. 590.

from favoring the "tough" political line of the Czechoslovak Party, made its leadership face unexpected problems at times, as it did, for instance, on the occasion of
reconciliation between the Kremlin and Tito's Yugoslavia in May, 1955. Czechoslovak information and
propagation media had continued relentlessly, long
after the death of Stalin, their massive attacks at the
regime of Marshal Tito, along the lines fixed by the
Cominform in 1948. The "mission of good will" of
Nikita S. Khrushchev to Belgrade, therefore, put the
Czechoslovak communists in a very awkward situation.
They chose to react by recording the event without
details or comment and by "enlightening" the top
Party cadres on its significance in secret meetings and
confidential circulars.[4] The same method was later
applied in analogous cases, whenever the Party leadership felt embarrassed by Soviet moves, for example
after the dissolution of the Cominform or in face of
the famous Khrushchev speech at the Twentieth CPSU
Congress, exposing "the excesses of the personality cult
era."[5]

The Echo of the Twentieth Congress of the CPSU in Czechoslovakia

It would seem that, with the onset of thaw in the
U.S.S.R., the Stalinist diehards in the leadership of the
Communist Party of Czechoslovakia had in turn to
re-evaluate their country's integration in the communist system in terms of benefit-cost analysis. However,
fairly narrow limits were set, from the beginning, for
an eventual revision of the "vertical" integrative rela-

[4] Cf. *Rudé právo* (Prague), August 12, 1964.
[5] Cf. *ibid.*

tionship to the Soviet power center. While Yugoslavia and later—though on entirely different grounds—Albania and China could openly defy Moscow because their communist parties were always conscious of the fact that their party states had come into existence without any notable help from the Soviet Union, the Stalinists in the Czechoslovak Party, were aware more than any other faction of the dependence of the Czechoslovak regime on the U.S.S.R. Their response to unwelcome trends in the communist system was therefore rather a slow and reluctant adjustment than an active opposition.

Notwithstanding the displeasure of the "dogmatic" cadres, the events of 1956 had a considerable response in Czechoslovakia. The message of the Twentieth Congress of the CPSU released a wave of daring criticism of the recent past. Artists, students, and intellectuals were the first spokesmen of this movement, which manifested itself strongly during the Second Congress of the National Union of Writers, held in Prague in April, 1956.[6] Lower Party units pressed the Secretariat and the Central Committee to convoke an extraordinary Party congress, but the leadership successfully resisted the pressure and contained the movement by a compromise solution in the form of a National Party Conference. This gathering, convened in Prague in May, 1956, consisted of the most docile elements of the regional and district organizations as selected by the First Secretary and in no way embarrassed the Party leadership. The delegates listened patiently, mostly *in*

---

[6] Cf. address by František Hrubín to the Second Czechoslovak National Writers Congress, as reproduced in *Literární noviny* (Prague), April 28, 1956; and speech at the same Congress by Jaroslav Seifert, as reproduced in *Literární noviny* (Prague), April 29, 1956.

camera, to the official presentation of the new Soviet policy line and received, in a limited number of copies, the expurgated translation of the speech N. Khrushchev had delivered February 24, 1956. The only concrete step in the direction of "repairing the mistakes of the personality-cult era" was the appointment by the Conference of a special fact-finding commission to investigate the accusations and verdicts in the past political trials. However, the fact that the commission was not instructed to examine the cogency of the processes which had taken place after 1952, rendered its task incomplete from the very begining. The work of the commission terminated in June, 1956, with a brief announcement that it "did not find anything irregular about the political trials up to 1952, except that the charge of 'titoism' had been unfounded in all cases." This verdict was a concession to the new Soviet foreign policy rather than to justice or to the victims. Nevertheless, some of the condemned persons were released, but not rehabilitated; in general, the press and radio ignored these amnesties.[7] As a token gesture of the verbally admitted need for "overcoming the evil consequences of the personality cult," the former Security Minister and Minister of Defense, Klement Gottwald's son-in-law Alexej Čepička, was removed from office and stripped of all his Party functions.

For the rest, the ferment in other party states, especially in the neighboring Hungary and Poland, was officially ignored. As it was gaining momentum, the

---

[7] Most defendants of the great political trials were released by the end of 1956 (Eduard Goldstücker, Arthur Gérard-London, Laco Novomeský, and others); only Gustav Husák, the chief defendant at the Bratislava trial against the "bourgeois nationalists," was held in prison until 1960; cf. Information Items, Radio Free Europe Archives, Munich 1956.

Czechoslovak authorities temporarily suspended import of publications from these two countries. The Hungarian uprising and the subsequent Soviet military intervention gave the Party a welcome pretext to stop all further moves towards "liberalization." On the whole, in 1956, the Communist Party of Czechoslovakia showed the symptoms of polycentrism, i.e., of the shift toward a more independent position within the communist party-state system and in relation to the U.S.S.R., in reverse: It tried to contain and delay the general trends of the thaw and destalinization. The temporary stiffening of the Soviet policy line after the dramatic events in Budapest not only restored, to a large extent, the harmony between the positions of the Soviet and Czechoslovak Parties; it also made the integration of Czechoslovakia appear more profitable in terms of political security to the advocates of the tough course in the CPCS.

Last Triumphs of Dogmatism

The continuation of Stalinist policies in Czechoslovakia beyond the 1956 mark was reflected not only in politics but also in the economy. It was only after 1956 that the collectivization drive in agriculture reached its peak, and it was not before 1960 that the process was concluded with about 90 percent of all arable land brought under administration by Uniform Agricultural Cooperatives or state farms.[8] The last vestiges of private trade and liberal professions disappeared. Artisans who conducted their trades unofficially at home were prosecuted by the law as "parasites" and "speculators."

[8] Cf. *Zemědělské noviny* (Prague), March 24, 1961.

In the intellectual sphere, several attempts were made to renew the conditions prevailing before 1956, i.e., to bring the arts and literature again under the complete control of the Party and to impose "socialist realism" upon all artists as an obligatory style. These efforts were only partly successful; the Party supervisors were able to stop the publication of works considered by them too "liberal," but they could no longer maintain their norm-setting power.[9] The atheist campaign was restarted with a new vigor in the late fifties, but its effectiveness appears mediocre if we read official comments dating from those years.[10]

The most conspicuous sign of the surviving "dogmatism" was the new Czechoslovak constitution of July, 1960. This document, superseding the first Communist Constitution promulgated in June, 1948, was Stalinist both in spirit and form: Not only did it take over entire passages from Stalin's Constitution of 1936 ("The Golden Book of Soviet Peoples") but, in certain

[9] One of the most talented Czech humorists of the younger generation, Josef Škvorecký, became the target of concentrated attacks by orthodox communists because of his autobiographic novel Zbabělci ("The Cowards"), published in 1958. The book describes the last week before the final collapse of the Nazi power in Bohemia, as seen through the eyes of a young man in a small East Bohemian town. The crime of Škvorecký was rather in what he did not say than in what he actually said: not a single word about the role and the merits of the Communist Party in the liberation of Czechoslovakia appeared in his book. His novel was confiscated and Škvorecký was expelled from his office in the Writers Union. Five years later, however, The Cowards was published in a second edition. Cf. the criticism of Škvorecký by the novelist Karel Nový in Rudé právo (Prague), Jan. 14, 1959.

[10] Pravda (Bratislava), Feb. 9, 1960; Predvoj (Bratislava), June 23, 1960; Rovnost (Brno), Oct. 15, 1959.

places, it surpassed it in dogmatic rigidity.[11] The 1960
Constitution changed the official title of Czechoslovakia to "The Czechoslovak Socialist Republic." This
change was ideologically motivated in the preamble,
which states that the building of socialism has been
completed in Czechoslovakia and that the country
stands now "on the threshold of communism."[12] Another
remarkable aspect of the 1960 Constitution is that it formally specifies the severe limitations to Slovak national
autonomy which had been practiced by the CPCS since
the 1948 coup d'état despite all formally valid agreements and legal regulations.[13] The new Constitution
curtailed the prerogatives of the Slovak regional parliament, the Slovak National Council, and abolished altogether the local government for Slovakia, the Board of
Commissioners. The constitutional reform of 1960 thus
reflected the fact that dogmatic thinking among the
Party leadership had maintained the upper hand.

The continuation of the conservative line in Czechoslovak domestic politics during the late fifties had
been to a certain extent favored by the contemporary
development in the communist system. The conference
of the Communist and Workers' Parties in Moscow, in
November, 1957, condemned Yugoslavia in strong
terms and declared revisionism to be the principal
danger threatening the world communist movement, a
clearly greater danger than dogmatism, which was denounced at the same time in the final resolution.[14]

[11] Cf. *Constitution of the Czechoslovak Socialist Republic; A
Background Report* (Munich: Radio Free Europe, 1960); see
also Zdenek Suda; "La nouvelle constitution tchécoslovaque,"
Est-&-Ouest (Paris), Oct. 1960, no. 243.
[12] Cf. *ibid.*
[13] Cf. *ibid.*
[14] Cf. *Declaration of the Conference of Communist and Workers Parties in Moscow*, Nov., 1957.

However, the trends manifest in the 1960 Constitution, especially the explicit claim that Czechoslovakia had "concluded the task of building socialism" and that it already stood "on the threshold of communism," again set the Czechoslovak party state apart from other smaller countries of the communist system. Also, while the new "left" radicalism in Czechoslovakia was in full swing, the general climate in the international communist movement underwent a new change. The conference of eighty-one communist parties in Moscow, in December, 1960, far from showing a united front against "revisionism," disclosed a deeply rooted disagreement on many basic points. At the subsequent Twenty-Second Congress of the Communist Party of the Soviet Union, in November, 1961, the rupture with Albania was completed. Polycentrism within the communist system gained a new momentum. At the same time, the scene was set for the second wave of destalinization. Czechoslovakia, for a number of reasons, was not to escape this one.

Integrative Trends during the Transitory Period

In the years following Stalin's death, the links between Czechoslovakia and other smaller countries of the communist system—their horizontal relations—became on the whole closer than before. The bilateral binding of Czechoslovakia to the Soviet Union continued also during this period, but it was no longer exclusive; it left more room for direct contacts to the other European party states. Though the only political cooperative organ, the Cominform, was dissolved in April, 1956, the intra-system exchanges became more frequent. We can affirm even more: It was precisely after the dissolution of the Information Bureau of the Communist and Workers' Parties that those parties started to be better informed about each other and to entertain direct relations. The conclusion sounds paradoxical, yet it is logical: In the given historical situation, polycentrism promoted integration—or, to say the least, it has been an incomparably lesser obstacle to the integrative process than the monopoly trend toward vertical relationships.

In its relations with the U.S.S.R. the Communist Party of Czechoslovakia steered a careful course and successfully avoided taking sides in the Soviet Party's inner struggle of 1957. All evidence points to the fact that the Czechoslovak communists had never completely trusted the solidity of the foundations of Khrushchev's policies and personal power. This may partly explain, proper allowance being made for their own interests and motives, the extremely cautious proceeding of the CPCS in the matter of destalinization. The Czechoslovak Socialist Republic aligned itself with Khrushchev's political views, especially in internal questions, only shortly before his downfall; it is very probable that other, more powerful motives prompted this alignment than the recognition by the Czechoslovak Party leadership of the correctness of the general guide lines put forward by the First Secretary of the CPSU. However, the loyalty of the Czechoslovak Communists to the Soviet Union could not be subject to any serious doubt—no more after the departure of Stalin than in Stalin's lifetime—although the Party leadership might have wished, on several occasions, that the Kremlin had chosen a different course.

In the military field, the post-Stalin era saw the first formal organizational link on the horizontal level among all party states in Central and Eastern Europe,

75

except Yugoslavia: The Warsaw Pact was signed in May, 1955. Politically, it was the response to West Germany's membership in NATO and in the West European Union. To a certain extent, it was supposed to be a counterpart of the Atlantic alliance, with its own integrated defense system countering the integrated defense system of the latter. The existence in its framework of a special Political Consultative Committee, which has been meeting at irregular intervals, seems to support this interpretation. The new pact, on the other hand, did not supersede the individual vertical defense treaties currently valid between the signatory states and the Soviet Union, but it provided a new basis, more in step with the age of peaceful coexistence, for keeping Soviet troops in East Germany, Hungary, Poland, and Rumania, especially after the evacuation of the Soviet occupation zone of Austria in September, 1955. It served also as a useful instrument of coordination of military policies and strategic planning.

This co-ordination, hitherto exclusively vertical, became operative also in the horizontal direction, but in the case of Czechoslovakia, the conclusion of the Warsaw Pact did not bring any revolutionary change. There had been no permanent Soviet garrisons stationed in Czechoslovakia since late 1945. On the other hand, the close co-operation of the Soviet military authorities with the Czechoslovak General Staff, indeed the direct supervision of the Czechoslovak armed forces by the Soviet military headquarters, had already previously assured a united high command and the standardization of weapons and military equipment. The two new elements in the situation were the activity of the Political Consultative Committee and occasional joint maneuvers of the armies of the Warsaw Pact countries.

The strengthening of the horizontal integrative tendencies could be observed also in the field of economy. On the whole, the increase of Czechoslovak foreign trade with the U.S.S.R. continued also during the post-Stalin years and maintained a greater rate of growth than the exchanges with other party states: Whereas the volume of the imports from and the exports to the Soviet Union doubled during the first seven years after Stalin's death, the trade with other people's democracies grew only by 58.5 percent.[15] However, even this increase was considerable and testified to an unprecedented intensification of the economic contacts between Czechoslovakia and the smaller party states of the system in Central and Eastern Europe.

Yet the most perceptible progress of the economic integration of Czechoslovakia into the communist system was achieved within the framework of the Council of Mutual Economic Aid (COMECON). Through this body, which kept its rather loose character without any permanent executive organ of its own, new institutional links were established among the member countries. At the tenth meeting of the COMECON in Prague, in 1958, an agreement was reached between the Soviet Union and four other signatory nations—Czechoslovakia, East Germany, Hungary and Poland—on the construction of an oil pipeline called *Druzhba* ("Friendship"). The project was completed in 1964. The "Friendship" pipeline transports crude oil from the Urals to Central Europe. The branch supplying Czechoslovakia and Hungary ends in Bratislava, where a large refinery was built as a Czechoslovak contribution to this multilateral project. Czechoslovakia did also bear the cost of the pipeline section situated on its territory; this cost amounted, according to official in-

[15] Cf. *The Statistical Yearbook 1960*, pp. 360–62.

formation, to 420 million Czechoslovak crowns (60 million dollars.)

Another important joint venture of the COMECON member states was the creation of a regional electricity grid which supplies Bulgaria, Czechoslovakia, East Germany, Hungary, Poland, Rumania, and the U.S.S.R. with electric energy. The project was approved at the 11th meeting of the Ministers of the COMECON countries in Tirana, in May, 1959. The official name of the grid is "The Central Organization of Rallied Energy Networks." As the title suggests, the set-up does not provide any additional, independent sources of electric power but rather pools the existing national capacities of the participating states. The central dispatching agency of the organization is seated in Prague. The grid became fully operative on January 1, 1963, but its further extension has been under study for a number of years.

During the transitory period, horizontal integration among the communist party states became also the subject of thorough theoretical studies. Czechoslovak communist economists played an important role in carrying out this task and in co-ordinating similar efforts of other theoreticians within the communist sphere.[16] On the initiative of the Czechoslovak Academy of Science, an international conference was convened at Liblice, near Prague, in 1957, the main topic of which was the analysis of the economic relationships

[16] Cf. J. Dudinski, "The Heavy Industry of the People's Democracies—Foundations of their Economic Might," *International Affairs* (Moscow), no. 7/55, August 1955; cf. also *Ekonomické vztahy mezi zeměmi socialistické světové soustavy* ("Economical Relations between the Countries of the Socialist Wrold System," a summary of the discussion at the international economic conference at Liblice, Czechoslovakia, in 1957) (Prague: SNPL Publishers, 1958).

among the countries of the World Socialist System. It is interesting to note that it was precisely about this time that the term "World Socialist System" appeared in the communist economic vocabulary. The term corresponds, almost exactly, to our notion of the communist party-state system. The conference of Liblice was attended by economists from practically all communist countries, including China. The same participation was registered at another meeting of this kind, convened in Prague in December, 1958. The central theme of this second conference was "the international division of labor in the World Socialist System." Though the international division of labor had not yet been understood in its special meaning, which will be discussed later on, all delegates agreed that economic relations among communist nations are of a special nature, determined by the social ownership of the means of production in every communist state, which, in the opinion of the speakers, precluded all exploitation also on the international level. Therefore, so argued the participants in the conference, "socialist states are predisposed to pursue close economic co-operation, a much closer one than any existing among countries outside the socialist system."[17] The foundations thus had been laid to an important integration movement, which, four years later, was launched within the sphere of COMECON.

In the later fifties, Czechoslovakia assumed a special role in implementing co-ordinated economic policies of the communist system. It became, next to the Soviet Union, the most important donor of foreign development credits and aid which it awarded not only to

[17] Cf. Vladimír Wacker-Bohumil Malý, *Mezinárodní socialistická dělba práce* ("International Socialist Division of Labor") (Prague: NPL Publishers, 1964), p. 25.

underdeveloped communist countries but also to the developing nations in Asia, Africa, and Latin America. This economic assistance, part of a carefully worked-out communist power strategy, reached record proportions of the equivalent of 30 U.S. dollars per capita per year. It surpassed several times the corresponding Soviet expenditure[18] and became soon a heavy burden for the Czechoslovak economy.

For example, in June, 1959, the Czechoslovak government granted a relatively large credit of 100 million old roubles (12 million dollars) to Albania. This money was supposed to finance the Albanian purchase of machinery and other finished products in Czechoslovakia.[19] The subsequent Soviet-Albanian split froze the major part of this Albanian debt. In the period from 1951 till 1955, Czechoslovakia awarded a development aid mounting to 160 million old roubles (20 million dollars) to Bulgaria.[20] Castro's Cuba received two loans in dollars from Czechoslovakia, 20 million each, partly interest-free, in 1960. In addition to these credits, another 23 million dollars' worth of capital investment goods was exported from Czechoslovakia to Cuba under special development aid agreements between the two countries.[21] In the beginning of the sixties, Czechoslovakia allowed large credits to the German Democratic Republic for the purpose of the development and the modernization of its chemical industry, chiefly

[18] Cf. *Pravda* (Bratislava), May 20, 1963; *Smena* (Bratislava), Dec. 24, 1963.

[19] Cf. *Pravda* (Bratislava), June 13, 1963; see also Zdenek Suda, "La Tchécoslovaquie et le blocus soviétique contre l'Albanie," *Est-&-Ouest* (Paris), Feb. 1962, no. 14, pp. 1–15.

[20] Cf. Radio Free Europe, Background Information, May 18, 1960.

[21] Cf. United Press International, release from June 11, 1960; *Zemědělské noviny* (Prague), Oct. 29, 1960.

of the plants producing artificial fertilizers.[22] The Korean People's Democratic Republic, in the years 1955–1960, received special economic and technical aid from Czechoslovakia on the basis of a treaty signed in December, 1954.[23] Czechoslovak specialists helped to build a large leather plant in Mongolia, in 1957, for which the Czechoslovak industry provided the necessary machinery. In 1961 Czechoslovakia opened a credit of 112.5 million new roubles (135 million dollars) to Poland.[24] Rumania received, in 1959, a long-term loan amounting to 60 million dollars in hard currency.[25] The Soviet Union was awarded by far the largest credits: In 1960, it received two billion Czechoslovak crowns (280 million dollars) worth capital investment for the purpose of intensive extracting of Soviet non-ferrous ores and, four years later, an undisclosed amount which was probably comparable to the first one, as the Czechoslovak contribution to the development of iron ore extraction in the U.S.S.R.[26] In May, 1962, the Democratic Republic of Vietnam signed a treaty with Czechoslovakia, according to which North Vietnam received complete investment units, such as shoe factories, tileworks, etc.[27] In the late fifties, Yugoslavia was granted 50 million dollars investment aid and 25 million dollars credit for the purchase of goods in hard currency markets.[28]

The money value of some special forms of aid—such as industrial blueprints, which, for a long time had

[22] Cf. *Rovnost* (Brno), Sept. 6, 1964.
[23] Cf. *Zahraniční obchod* (Prague), June 1959.
[24] Cf. *Czechoslovak Economic Bulletin* (Prague), no. 8, 1957, Aug. 1957.
[25] Cf. Rumanian Home Radio Service, Oct. 3, 1959.
[26] Cf. Radio Prague, Sept. 28, 1966.
[27] Cf. *Rudé právo* (Prague), May 5, 1962.
[28] Cf. *Rudé právo* (Prague), December 21, 1958.

been given free to other COMECON states—is not included in the above figures. The great majority of credits awarded by Czechoslovakia to other communist countries was repayable in kind, mostly in the form of deliveries of raw materials.[29] The credits and aid received by Czechoslovakia from other party states cannot compare to the value of its own foreign help expenditures. According to reliable sources, in the period from 1956 through 1960, Czechoslovakia had been awarded by other communist countries, chiefly by the U.S.S.R., credits amounting to about 500 million dollars. During the same time, Czechoslovakia spent on credits and development grants to the rest of the communist party states the sum of no less than 1.2 billion dollars.[30] The official information sources admitted an event greater disproportion: The relation of the help given to the help received was three to one![31]

The Belated "Thaw"

The advancing trend towards polycentrism—in itself an anti-Stalinist factor—made it possible, paradoxically enough, for the Czechoslovak leadership to hold back the wave of destalinization for a considerable length of time ' because it lowered the pressure for uniformity within the communist party state system. The actual thaw set in only in the early sixties. It is probable that it would have been still later in coming, had not serious economic difficulties sped up the process. This crisis was area-wide: Since 1961, a general slow-down in the production growth and economic development had

[29] Cf. *Hospodářské noviny* (weekly), (Prague), April 29, 1966.
[30] Cf. *New York Times*, Feb. 2, 1961.
[31] Cf. *Pravda* (Bratislava), May 5, 1963.

been observed in all communist countries in Central
and Eastern Europe, except in Rumania. In Czechoslovakia it became particularly severe. Almost none of
the target figures of the economic plan for 1961 was
reached, neither in industry nor in agriculture, so that
the Third Five-Year Plan (1959–1963) had to be scrapped. Since then the Czechoslovak economy has been
managed on the basis of short-term one-year plans.[32]
The effects of the crisis were soon felt in the distribution. An acute shortage of commodities of all kind
arose, reminding the population of the conditions in
the fifties, before the monetary reform. It was clear to
many leading communists that the Stalinist national
economy had had its day.

Because of the close association between economic
and political Stalinism, it was impossible to attack the
first without criticizing the second. Hence the opponents of the dogmatic line in politics, culture, and
justice acquired a powerful ally among the partisans of
economic destalinization. At the same time, they began
to obtain substantial support from the upcoming generation of the Party élites, whose record was free of
any responsibility for the "excesses of the personality-
cult era" and who therefore had no reason to fear any
thorough revision of the hitherto accepted Party policies. The liberalization drive in Czechoslovakia thus
gained its own momentum, independent of the currents prevailing in the communist system.

The events in the international communist movement in the early sixties, however, were not entirely

[32] Cf. the statement of the Central Committee of the CPCS,
O výhledech dalšího rozvoje naší socialistické společnosti ("On
the Prospects of Further Development of Our Socialist Society"),
published as a supplement to the daily *Rudé právo* (Prague),
Aug. 14, 1962, p. 4.

without consequence for Czechoslovakia. The break between the Soviet Union and Albania, made public at the Twenty-Second Congress of the CPSU in Moscow in October, 1961, was a prelude to the Sino-Soviet split and could not but weaken the position of those in the Party leadership who advocated the continuation of the old policy line. The issue of the Soviet dispute with Albania and, later, with China, was—or at least was claimed to be—the choice between Stalinism and pure Leninism, in other words, between dogmatism and a mild, Soviet brand of revisionism. Whoever, under these conditions, adopted or maintained dogmatic policies, exposed himself to the danger of implicitly becoming an ally of China and Albania against the Soviet Union. This, for reasons already given, was unimaginable to the Czechoslovak communists. For the second time since the death of Stalin, the integration of Czechoslovakia in the communist party-state system proved to be a fact fostering the thaw.

The door was thus open to a new wave of "destalinization," much more powerful than that which Czechoslovakia had experienced in 1956. The official signal to the destalinization campaign was given at the Twelfth Congress of the CPCS in December, 1962. Already in the months immediately preceding the supreme Party convention, the outward symbols of the Stalinist era were rapidly disappearing. Street names were changed, the oversized statue of the deceased Kremlin dictator was demolished in Prague. Though the top leaders, in their comments on the personality cult presented during the Congress, tried to reconcile the usual interpretation of the political trials of the fifties with the requirements of the thaw, their general retreat was obvious. A new fact-finding commission was set up to investigate the charges brought against the defendants of these processes. This time, in contrast with the decision of the National Party Conference in 1956, all trials including those of 1953 and 1954 were put on the agenda of the Commission. The Commission made public its findings on August 22, 1963.[33] It established that, from the point of view of pure law, none of the indictments could be upheld and that, consequently, all defendants had been innocent. The formal rehabilitation through a decree of the Ministry of Justice followed immediately upon the Committee's report. This decision was, of course, inconceivable without simultaneously exposing the culprits. The Public Attorney who had conducted the preliminary investigations and had represented the Party and the State at the show trials, Josef Urválek, was dismissed from his function as early as in the spring of 1962, along with the First Secretary of the Slovak Communist Party, Karol Bacílek. Bacílek was held responsible by the Slovak press for having fabricated the charges of "an imaginary bourgeois nationalism." The same responsibility was attributed by the Slovak Communists to the CPS Chairman Viliam Široký,[34] who lost all his Party and State appointments after the rehabilitation of the victims of the Stalinist justice. The purge which brought about his fall affected several members of the Old Guard in the Party leadership, both Czechs and Slovaks.[35] Among the leaders of long standing, only the First Secretary Antonín Novotný was able to keep his functions. The expelled officials were replaced, almost exclusively, by Party apparatus people of the younger

[33] Press release of Czechoslovak Press Agency ČETEKA, Aug. 22, 1963.
[34] Cf. *Pravda* (Bratislava), June 3, 1963.
[35] Cf. *Rudé právo* (Prague), Sept. 22, 1963.

generation who were unsoiled by the "misdeeds of the personality-cult era."

The rehabilitation of the Communist leaders who had been tried in the fifties, however, was not consistent: None of the surviving defendants of the great show-trials was restored to the office previously held in the CPCS or in the government. This was, above all, the case of the Slovak "bourgeois nationalists." Their qualified rehabilitation can be considered as a successful maneuver on the part of the First Secretary Antonín Novotný, whose situation would have been very awkward if he had had to face, in the highest Party councils, the comrades for whose unjust sentencing he had been largely responsible. On the other hand, the failure to satisfy fully the demands of the Slovak communists had serious consequences. The Slovak Party cadres became embittered not only because of the refusal on the part of the leadership to reinstate the "bourgeois nationalists" in their old positions but also on account of the rigid centralist policies of the Prague Secretariat, which continued, even after the rehabilitation of the defendants, to ignore the ethnic demands of the Slovak people. In the years following the Twelfth Congress, continuous unrest among the Slovak intelligentsia worried considerably the chiefs of the CPCS. Some limited effort was made by them to accommodate Slovak national aspirations by a relative increase of the Slovak National Council's domain in administrative and economic matters; however, since none of the proposed reforms aimed at the root of the discontent, the ruthless centralism embodied in the 1960 Constitution, they did not have any notable effect.[36] Destalinization as such, it was obvious, did not facilitate the solution

[36] Cf. *Rudé právo* (Prague), May 8, 1964.

of the most important integration problem on the national level in Czechoslovakia.

After the Twelfth Party Congress, critical voices in the daily press and in some periodicals, especially in cultural and literary reviews, became loud and daring. In their boldness they soon surpassed anything that had been written in Czechoslovakia during the short liberalization episode in 1956.

Despite the disapproval of the regime and its repeated attempts to curb the newly acquired freedom (for example, by the special resolution on the tasks and responsibilities of the Socialist press, voted at the subsequent Thirteenth Party Congress in June, 1966; or by the new press law, enacted by the National Assembly in October, 1966; or by stringent Party-discipline measures against communist writers and intellectuals in the summer and fall of 1967) the movement could not be contained. On the contrary, the steps which were supposed to put an end to the "rebellion on the cultural front" proved to be a boomerang, fatal to First Secretary Novotný and his group. The resistance of Czech and Slovak artistic and literary circles to political control was one of several factors which eventually brought about the downfall of the whole Party leadership and produced a new, third wave of "liberalization," unprecedented in the whole history of not only communist Czechoslovakia but the entire communist party-state system.

5: ON THE EVE OF
THE GREAT CHANGE

Though the second de-Stalinization move which started at the Twelfth Party Congress in December, 1962, did not meet the expectations of the partisans of a more "liberal" course, it cannot be said that it remained limited to the revision of some political trials and to the cleaning of tarnished public symbols. Since it had been prompted, to a large extent, by economic difficulties, it was only natural that its impact proved particularly strong in the national economy. In the field of economic theory it gave a powerful impulse to new, unorthodox ways of thinking, which at present are being described by the general term of "economic revisionism."

Already long before December, 1962, there had been an opinion gaining ground among the top functionaries in industry and among Party economists that the entrenched system of operating on the basis of a plan that was explicit to the smallest details and that reduced the actual production and distribution units to the role of passive recipients of orders from above was responsible for the unsatisfactory functioning of the Czechoslovak economy. This awkward and ineffective type of economic organization was a legacy of the Stalinist period. At the Twelfth Party Congress, a resolution was voted which advised the Central Committee

89

to seek ways and means of adapting the national economy to the "conditions of the advanced stage of socialist development."[1] This was more or less a green light to "economic revisionism."

The New Economic Model

However, it took almost three years to prepare a blueprint for the economic reform. In its final form, approved by the Thirteenth Party Congress in June, 1966, the plan turned out to be a compromise among many views, including the views of influential conservative members of the Party leadership.[2] Tests on a small scale had been carried out for about a year before the project went into full application on January 1, 1967.

The improved economic system aimed at by the reformers carried the official designation "the New Economic Model." It signified the return to the market principle in a considerable degree, i.e., to the recognition of the law of supply and demand; it also took into consideration "natural" factors in economic life, such as the drive for profit and higher income, which have been ignored by the orthodox communist economic theory. Moreover, it loosened the inflexible and cumbersome methods of planning on a centralized basis.

In the framework of the New Economic Model, the long-term centralist planning is to be limited to the setting-up of the so-called "basic targets," i.e., the

[1] Cf. Resolution of the Twelfth Congress of the CPCS, *Rudé právo* (Prague), Dec. 10, 1962.

[2] Cf. Resolution of the Thirteenth Congress of the CPCS, as a special supplement to the daily *Rudé právo* (Prague), June 7, 1966.

volume of investment and of production in the sectors of heavy industry, raw materials, and energy. All other economic planning is to be made for the maximum period of one year, by industrial units of the medium and lower grades (the managements of enterprises and subsidiaries). Prices are to be gradually freed and exposed to the direct effect of the situation on the market. Only the prices of raw materials, of energy, and of imported capital investment goods shall continue to be regulated by the government, while those of basic commodities (chiefly foodstuffs) are to be subject to administrative controls (ceiling prices).

In order to increase the productivity of labor, the New Economic Model has introduced the notion of "material incentives," or, in the communist economic terminology, the notion of the "material interest of the workers in the economic results of the enterprise." The previous system of wages and bonuses, based upon the percentage of the fulfillment of the plan targets, is to be gradually replaced by a much simpler mechanism of remunerating the employees in proportion to the profit which the plant will realize. The managements of individual production units are allowed considerable freedom in fixing the prices of their products and thus in assuring the profitability of their enterprises, but they have to take into consideration the overall situation on the market, i.e., eventual competition from other producers in the same branch.[3] A progressive "de-nivellization" or re-differentiation of the pay scales, is to accompany this reform of the wages and salaries system. Skilled workers, employees with higher

[3] Cf. Ota Šik, *K problematice socialistických zbožních vztahů* ("On the Problems of Socialist Market Relations"), (Prague: Czechoslovak Acadamy of Science, 1965); cf. also *Die tschecholowakische Wirtschaft auf neuen Wegen* (Prague: Orbis, 1966).

education, and specialists are to receive substantially higher pay than unskilled labor; hitherto, the difference in the remuneration has been only very slight. The same principles are to be applied also in the agriculture, though the New Economic Model will require adapting to the special conditions of rural economy.

These reforms, if carried out consistently, cannot fail to affect the political set-up. They postulate, by implication, the surrender by the Party of the economic monopoly, that was an indispensable condition for the maintenance of its absolute power. The authors and the advocates of the New Economic Model have been well aware of the necessity to reform the "political model," too.[4] It was on their initiative that, following a resolution of the Thirteenth Party Congress, a special commission began to examine this problem. Later, in the course of the application of the economic reform, the imperatives of a better working economy came in a sharp conflict with the vested political interests of the Party leadership and triggered off, along with other factors, the third and the most dramatic phase of "liberalization."

The new course in economy, embarked upon by the CPCS, is not a Czechoslovak specialty. By 1967, almost all Communist party states in Central and Eastern Europe have adopted similar measures, though these vary in their extent and intensity.[5] However, the Czech-

[4] Cf. the report by Ota Šik, presented at the Thirteenth Congress of the CPCS, as recorded in *Rudé právo* (Prague), on June 5, 1966.

[5] Cf. Harry Trend and Dorothy Miller, "The East German Economic Reforms," in *Problems of Communism* (Washington), March-April, 1966; cf. also the documents on the Soviet economic reform measures, as reproduced in *Ost-Probleme* (Bad Godesberg, West Germany), Nov. 5, 1965.

oslovak New Economic Model has the best theoretical foundation; there is a whole school of economic thought behind it. Also, it is much more radical than, for example, the comparable project which is being applied in the U.S.S.R. Thus the economic reform, while it stresses the similarity between Czechoslovakia and certain other party states in Central and Eastern Europe, magnifies the difference between Czechoslovakia and the Soviet Union. Moreover, if we consider that the "economic revisionism" has been among the leading forces of the Czechoslovak "liberalization" movement, with its disturbing consequences in the sphere of intra-system relations, we have to conclude that the New Economic Model is hardly an element promoting system integration.

The Most Ambitious Attempt at Area Integration

Stalin's successors realized that the cohesion of the communist party-state system could no longer be based upon Soviet dictate but that a minimum of consensus would have to be secured from the individual ruling parties. For this reason, the only instrument of integration on hand at the time, the Cominform, was repudiated in 1956; in the minds of the élites of the smaller communist countries it was too closely associated with the period of undisguised Soviet domination. However, the Soviet leaders have never ceased seeking new ways of transforming the former monolithic bloc into a coordinated unit capable of appearing as a homogenous body in the arena of international politics. It has not been possible, until the present day, to say whether there is any chance for these efforts to succeed.

The Soviet Union has tried several avenues of approach to the solution of this problem. In the first half of the sixties, two attempts at integration on a regional scale in Central and Eastern Europe were made by the CPSU leadership. The initiative launched by Nikita Khrushchev within the framework of the Council of Mutual Economic Assistance was the most important of the two. By means of a close co-ordination of planning and investment policies and by means of an advanced specialization of production among the member-states, the entire area of COMECON was to be molded into one self-sufficient economic unit, with inevitable political consequences. It was this method that was referred to under the special name of "the international socialist division of labor."

The term was not entirely new: The international socialist division of labor appears as early as 1955 in the analyses of Soviet economists and in the writings of theoreticians in other communist countries.[6] However, in the beginning it was understood to be a rather spontaneous process taking place among all communist party states, whether they were members of the COMECON or not, a process which merited encouragement but did not require any special management. Even when it appeared on the agenda of COMECON meetings (as, for instance, in Moscow in June, 1958, where it figured as the main subject for discussion)[7] or of international economic conferences (such as the meeting of the communist economists in Prague, in

---

[6] Cf. J. Dudinski, "The Heavy Industry of the People's Democracies"; cf. *Rozvoj mezinárodní dělby práce v socialistické světové soustavě* (Development of the International Socialist Division of Labor in the World Socialist System") (summary of the international economic conference held in Prague, December 15–16, 1958), (Prague: SNPL Publishers, 1959).

[7] Cf. *Pravda* (Moscow), May 24, 1958.

December, 1958), it did not differ much from the current notion of the international division of labor[8] except for the fact that it was supposed to be limited to economic relations among communist countries. It was only in the early sixties that the term was given a new substance. At the fifteenth session of the COMECON in Warsaw, in December, 1961, and at a special meeting of the communist parties' heads of the COMECON member countries in Moscow, in June, 1962, the international socialist division of labor was launched as a project based upon a definite and detailed pre-established plan. The concrete targets of this project were described in a document called *The Principles of the International Socialist Division of Labor,* and the highest convention of the communist functionaries in Moscow approved and promulgated it in a solemn way.[9]

The *Principles,* along with several commentaries by communist theoreticians and party leaders and especially the article which Nikita Khrushchev himself wrote for the "World Marxist Review,"[10] reveal the ambitious nature of the project, as it aims at economic integration on a supranational level. If the international socialist division of labor could have been achieved in the form postulated by the *Principles,* the national economies of the COMECON countries would have grown into an organic whole, a "universal socialist cooperative," as Mr. Khrushchev himself had put it.[11] The *Principles* suggested two chief methods of

[8] Cf. *Rozvoj mezinárodní dělby práce v socialistické světové soustavě,* as above.

[9] Cf. *Pravda* (Moscow), June 7, 1962.

[10] Cf. Nikita Khrushchev, "The Present Problems of the World Socialist System," *World Marxist Review* (Prague), Sept. 1962.

[11] Cf. *ibid.*

reaching this goal: the co-ordination of planning and the specialization of production. Both were to be developed on an area-wide scale. The COMECON member states were expected to specialize in the production of those kinds of goods which appeared to be the most rational in the given conditions—in view of the proximity of raw material sources, of cheapness or high productivity of labor, etc. Unprofitable production operations were to be transferred to other member countries where more advantageous conditions prevailed, or abandoned altogether. The *Principles* were supposed to apply to both industry and agriculture.

The realization of a project like this, which involved radical interventions in the domain of the participating national economies, was inconceivable without appropriate instruments. The co-ordination of capital investment and of the production plans, as well as the managing of the complicated process of specialization within the COMECON area, required new organs on the area level. These bodies—or this body—could not fulfill these tasks to satisfaction unless vested with the necessary authority to decide all the intricate issues in connection with the attribution of specialized production roles to different countries, and to settle eventual disputes among them. In other words, such a new organ would have to be endowed with supranational powers. It is probable that this aspect of the international socialist division of labor appeared particularly attractive to Khrushchev. The supranational organ postulated by the project promised to be an excellent agent of cohesion among the communist party states in Central and Eastern Europe.

Officially, of course, it has never been presented as a means of increasing the political unity of the COMECON region. According to Czechoslovak sources, the idea of the international socialist division of labor was of Polish origin and the purpose of the planned operation was to overcome the "crisis of growth" of the individual COMECON member countries, by pooling their economic resources.[12] Even when talking about the proposed supranatural co-ordinating body, Mr. Khrushchev justified the proposal by the necessity "to resolve the problems of co-ordination of the economic development of the socialist system."[13] However, the idea of a special regional planning board placed above the national economic authorities, which the Soviet delegation submitted at the seventeenth meeting of the COMECON in Bucharest, in December, 1962, was rejected. The most determined opposition against the Soviet initiative was shown on the part of Rumania.[14] Deprived of the indispensable instrument of co-ordination, the project of the international socialist division of labor could not make much headway. Its partial success, as measured thus far, has been almost exclusively on a bilateral basis.

The Czechoslovak Party leadership gave loyal support to the project from its beginning. It was evident that a consequent implementation of the *Principles* would have made the predominantly industrial COMECON countries, such as Czechoslovakia, into super-industrial powers, while it would have accentuated strongly the rural character of countries like Rumania. Therefore it might seem that Czechoslovakia could only draw benefits from an intensive division of labor

[12] Cf. Vladimír Wacker and Bohuslav Malý, *Mezinárodní socialistická dělba práce*, pp. 20–23.

[13] Cf. the speech by Nikita Khrushchev, at the meeting of the Central Committee of the CPSU, as reported by the press agency TASS, Moscow, Nov. 19, 1962.

[14] Cf. *Borba* (Belgrade), December 30, 1962.

97

among communist party states and that the Party's favorable opinion on the project should reflect, more or less, the opinion of the economic cadres. In reality, the idea of the international socialist division of labor has not met with unanimous approval in Czechoslovakia. The resistance against the project has been milder than, for example, in Rumania, but the official information media several times reported "unrest in the plants" and complained about "incorrect attitudes" of the managers in face of concrete measures, for example, the closing of factories or their transfer, required by the process of specialization.[15]

The difference of opinion on the international socialist division of labor between the Party leaders and the economic managers never matured into an open conflict because the original ambitious project was shelved. It is probable that its eventual realization would not have been very easy for Czechoslovakia. Many Czechoslovak economists were skeptical about the willingness of the other party states to bring the sacrifices necessary to the specialization and to the creation of an area-wide market; they feared that, when faced with a choice between the purchase of a COMECON article and an article from a third country, the Communist nations would follow their own particular interests. The critics of the proposed operation saw their fears confirmed when, at the turn of 1967, the U.S.S.R. and Bulgaria concluded a deal with the West European car manufacturers "Fiat" and "Renault" with the view of producing automobiles in these two countries, disregarding the previous COMECON agreement which had encouraged Czechoslovakia to develop assembly-line construction of the "Škoda" passenger

[15] Cf. Zdenek Suda, *La division internationale socialiste du travail* (Leyden: A. W. Sijthoff, 1967), pp. 98–99.

car MB 1000 as the "Volkswagen of the Socialist countries."[16]

An even more important obstacle to economic integration of Czechoslovakia on the area level arose in the form of the New Economic Model. The Czechoslovak economic reforms, too, required changes in the industrial structure—increase or reduction in the productive potential and transfer or abolition of the existing capacities. However, these reforms were conceived for domestic needs, on a strictly national level. Consequently, a production unit or branch considered superfluous or unprofitable from the regional point of view might very well justify its existence within the framework of the national economy, and vice versa. International specialization, as it was foreseen by the project of the international socialist division of labor, could very easily come into conflict with the requirements of the New Economic Model. Besides, the Czechoslovak economic reforms, which restore, to a large extent, the freedom of the industrial managers to purchase raw materials where they find the most advantageous offer and to sell their finished products where they obtain the most favorable price, break up the regional pattern of markets and weaken the integration links among the COMECON countries.

Czechoslovakia participated in several bilateral ventures, in the framework of the reduced project of the international socialist division of labor, for example in the joint production of tractors with Poland.[17] It became also a member of all the new agencies which were created by the COMECON in the first half of the

[16] Cf. Dr. Bruno Šteiner, "Tvrdá slova" ("Harsh Words"), Svět motorů (Prague), Nov. 1966, no. 22, pp. 14–15.
[17] Cf. Zdenek Suda, La division internationale, p. 56.

sixties. In 1963, the Organization for Co-operation in the Industry of Ball-Bearings was set up, which includes Bulgaria, Czechoslovakia, East Germany, Hungary, Poland and the U.S.S.R. The purpose of this body is to remedy the shortage of ball bearings in the communist countries, which was most acute in the years during and after the Korean war, as a consequence of the Western embargo on strategic goods and raw materials. In 1964 Czechoslovakia, Hungary, and Poland founded the "Intermetall," a clearing-house open to other COMECON countries, which gathers data and information on metal production in the signatory states and makes propositions to the individual governments concerning production plans, in view of the situation prevailing on the communist markets. The functions of both organizations are purely consultative.[18]

The most important COMECON creation in the sphere of transport is the Common Railroad Wagon Pool in which Czechoslovakia and all other member states, with the exception of Albania, participate. The Wagon Pool came into existence in 1964, in implementation of the agreement signed in December, 1963. It facilitates the joint use of the rolling-stock of the railroads in the COMECON area, to an extent which the previous international arrangement, R.I.V. (Regolamento Internazionale dei Veicoli), of 1921 did not allow. On the other hand, the stipulations of the Common Railroad Wagon Pool are neither so liberal nor so flexible as those of the West European Wagon Pool created in 1952 on the initiative of the Council of Europe.[19]

Czechoslovakia also became a founding member of

[18] Cf. *Hutnik* (monthly), (Prague), No. 9/1964, Sept. 1964, pp. 454–56.
[19] Cf. Zdenek Suda, *La division internationale*, pp. 52–53.

the International Bank for Economic Co-operation in Moscow. The treaty establishing the Bank was approved at the sixteenth meeting of the COMECON in Bucharest, in December, 1962. All COMECON countries except Albania are participating in the operations of this monetary institute. The Bank which began functioning on January 1, 1964, has considerably facilitated the trade exchanges between the signatory states, as it removed the awkward barter practices and the need to settle the clearing points in hard currencies. Every member country of the International Bank for Economic Co-operation keeps an open account at the institute which is expressed in "convertible roubles." The credits accumulated by exports to one member-state can be used to settle the debits caused by imports from any other signatory country. In case of an overall deficit in foreign trade, the country in question can apply for a short term loan from the Bank. However, the convertibility of the "convertible" rouble is strictly limited to the rouble zone, which itself does not even include all communist party states. Thus, for instance, the business transactions with Cuba and Yugoslavia continue to be carried out on the basis of American dollars. The International Bank for Economic Co-operation in no way solves Czechoslovakia's most important payment problem: the shortage of Western currencies essential for the purchase of many indispensable raw materials.[20]

In the sixties, several other, less important specialized agencies came into existence within the framework or on the initiative of the COMECON. Czechoslovakia has been party to most of them.[21] These organizations, like those which we have mentioned above,

[20] Cf. *ibid.*, pp. 59–61.
[21] Cf. *ibid.*, pp. 49–61.

are of a strictly international and consultative character. None of them can be therefore considered a substitute for the rejected central planning and co-ordination board which the Soviet Union had wanted to set up in the process of the international socialist division of labor. Nor did organizational changes in the structure of the COMECON, introduced in 1963— particularly the constitution of a permanent Executive Committee—modify its strictly international character and the need for all decisions to be made unanimously.[22] Economic integration on a supranational level has remained, so far, an unattained target of the radical school of economic thought in the communist party-state system.

During the period which we can call "pre-January"— that is, shortly before the spectacular change in the Czechoslovak CP leadership and policies in January, 1968—economic relations between Czechoslovakia and the remaining communist countries continued to develop on the familiar pattern. Trade with the U.S.S.R. maintained its predominant place, representing 36.9 percent of the total 1965 turnover.[23] Trade with the rest of the COMECON area held the second place with 31.2 percent.[24] However, during the last years, the proportion of trade with the Soviet Union and the people's democracies in the Czechoslovak foreign trade set-up has notably slowed down in its original rapid increase. Judging by previous experience, Czechoslovak economists had originally anticipated that the Soviet-Czechoslovak exchange of goods would reach, in 1965, 41.8 percent, and trade with the Communist countries

[22] Cf. *Rudé právo* (Prague), June 9, 1962.
[23] Cf. *The Statistical Yearbook 1966*, p. 426.
[24] Cf. *ibid.*, p. 426.

in Central and Eastern Europe, excluding the U.S.S.R., 38.2 percent of the total turnover.[25]

Czechoslovakia has carried on, in the role assumed in the fifties, as the banker of the underdeveloped communist nations. In 1966, for example, it granted a loan to the Soviet Union, amounting to 4 billion Czechoslovak crowns (560 million U.S. dollars). These funds are to be spent on the modernization and the expansion of the installation in the oil fields in West Siberia. The debtor is expected to repay the loan in crude oil deliveries, 14.5 million tons per year, beginning in 1970.[26] These investments, if carried out according to the agreement, are likely to determine the orientation of Czechoslovak fuel imports for many years to come, regardless of the intentions of the present liberal Party leadership. Czechoslovakia concluded a treaty with North Vietnam in January, 1966, which provides for financial aid amounting to 135 million crowns (19 million U.S. dollars) and for the training by Czechoslovak specialists of no less than two thousand skilled industrial workers. Since the escalation of the Vietnam war, the aid to North Vietnam has become increasingly "integrated." According to official statistics, Czechoslovakia, in cooperation with six other communist party states—Bulgaria, China, Hungary, Poland, Rumania, and the U.S.S.R.—provided loans, grants, and free deliveries of goods totaling, in 1966, 295 million new roubles (320 million dollars.)[27]

Trade with non-communist countries has grown, though not very fast. The lowest point seems to have

[25] Cf. *Tvorba* (Prague), vol. 1961, no. 18 (April 4, 1961); cf. also Radio Prague, Jan. 12, 1959.

[26] Cf. *Radio Free Europe Background Information*, Sept. 26 and Sept. 28, 1966.

[27] Cf. Radio Prague, Oct. 15, 1966.

been definitely overcome but the intensity of Czechoslovak economic relations with the Free World cannot yet compare to the conditions prevailing in the years before the coup d'état and immediately after it. In 1966, for example, exports to and imports from the states outside the communist system equaled about 30 percent of the foreign trade turnover.[28] A lively discussion has been going on for a considerable time among the economists and politicians on the possibility of strengthening these relations. The issue became particularly topical under the impact of the Rumanian example. Many theoreticians claimed that, since the creation of a separate, self-sufficient communist economic community by means of the international socialist division of labor had failed, Czechoslovakia should find its way back into the world economic system as soon as possible and participate fully in the division of labor among all nations of the earth.[29] The criticism of the one-sided orientation of Czechoslovak foreign trade thus dates from the period before January, 1968, though the democratization wave launched by the new Party leading team gave it a strong momentum and made the revision of hitherto valid principles a practical alternative.

Military and Political Integrative Trends 1963–1967

Another field in which Stalin's successors have attempted to strengthen the cohesion of the communist party states in Central and Eastern Europe has been the military system. The organization of the Warsaw

[28] Cf. Prokop Macháň, "Czechoslovak Foreign Trade," Radio Free Europe Archives, Munich, 1966.
[29] Cf. Radio Prague, Jan. 12, 1967.

Pact appeared to Nikita Khrushchev, and later to the Brezhnev-Kosygin team, as a suitable means to achieve closer co-ordination of military policies among the member countries, with the desired political side-effects.

Though the Soviet Union has enjoyed a privileged position in the Warsaw alliance—for example, all commanders-in-chief have always been Soviet officers—the treaty as such has kept its clearly international character. It requires that all decisions should be taken unanimously. The Warsaw Pact has two organs in which questions of common interest are discussed: the Conference of Defense Ministers and the Political Consultative Committee. The Conference of Defense Ministers meets at irregular intervals and relatively seldom; the most important session of this "ad hoc" body was held February 28, 1963, when "strengthening of the co-operation among the member states, by means of regular consultations" was agreed upon.[30] The Political Consultative Committee, following this decision, met in July, 1963, in January, 1965, in July, 1966, in February, 1967, and in March 1968. Joint maneuvers of the Warsaw Pact troops were held in October, 1965, in the East German province of Thuringia, under the code name "October Storm," and in September, 1966, in Bohemia, under the name "Vltava" ("The Moldau").

The idea to make the Warsaw Pact Treaty into an instrument of supranational regional integration was formulated by Mr. Khrushchev during his visit in Budapest, in April, 1964.[31] It did not make much progress, as several signatory states, in the first place Rumania and Poland, voiced their objections against

[30] Cf. *Rudé právo* (Prague), March 1, 1963.
[31] Cf. *Népszabadság* (Budapest), April 4, 1964.

the proposed abolition of the unanimity vote. The subsequent probing of the Kremlin, especially in summer, 1966, did not meet with a greater response than the previous advances. However, on the part of the Czechoslovak Party leadership, it seemed to have met with a positive reception.

The Soviet-Czechoslovak Treaty of Friendship, Mutual Assistance, and Postwar Co-operation of 1943 was renewed, in December, 1963, for another twenty years. While this bilateral link has been upheld, a certain de-sovietization took place in the inner structure of the Czechoslovak Army. In 1962, Soviet military ranks and distinctions were abolished and the army returned to the nomenclature current in the pre-communist period. In 1964, the Soviet-style uniforms were replaced by military clothing cut on the American pattern, which was found to be more practical by the official commentators.[32] Military co-operation with the U.S.S.R. and the other communist party states has never been very popular in Czechoslovakia. For example, at the occasion of the Warsaw Pact troops exercise "Vltava," in summer, 1966, the Slovak paper *Smena* reported that "disapproving voices have been heard among the population. People have been arguing that such operations are a luxury, a drain on the nation's resources, and that they should be postponed until the situation of the Czechoslovak economy improves."[33] And the Bratislava evening paper *Večerník* put it even more bluntly, saying that "the strength of the armed forces should be reduced" and that the Czechoslovak armaments are "too costly."[34] Similar

[32] Cf. *Pravda* (Bratislava), May 23, 1966; cf. also *Obrana lidu* (Prague), April 1, 1962.
[33] *Smena* (Bratislava), Aug. 25, 1966.
[34] *Večerník* (Bratislava), Aug. 25, 1966.

opinion could often be read in the Czechoslovak press, long before the suspension of advance censorship in the spring of 1968.

Formal de-sovietization was carried out also in the universities. In April, 1966, the system of academic degrees introduced in the early fifties, patterned on the Soviet model, was abolished and replaced by traditional Czechoslovak academic titles.

The trend toward less dependence on the Soviet power center was also perceptible in the sphere of foreign relations. In the second half of the sixties, direct political contacts have been made between Czechoslovakia and the Western powers, with Western politicians officially visiting Czechoslovakia and communist functionaries traveling on state visits to Western countries. Though many of these trips did not go beyond courtesy gestures and diplomatic routine, some contacts led to serious negotiations with definite objectives in view. Such was the case of the talks between the Czechoslovak government and a West German delegation in Prague, early in 1967, on the subject of establishing regular diplomatic relations with the German Federal Republic. At this juncture, the Soviet Union exerted considerable effort to influence and co-ordinate the policies of the communist party states in Central and Eastern Europe concerning relations with West Germany. A special conference was called in Warsaw in February, 1967, where Czechoslovakia, East Germany, and Poland took the pledge not to change their relations to the German Federal Republic without previous mutual consultation. Thus the so-called Iron Triangle came into existence. Despite this restriction, contacts on governmental level were established between Czechoslovakia and its Western neighbor with the exchange of Trade Missions in early 1968. Resumption of full diplomatic relations has been under discussion ever since that time, and became one of the key issues of Czechoslovak foreign policy in the eight months period of the liberalization experiment, before the Soviet intervention.

On the other hand, the loyal attitude of the Czechoslovak leadership towards the Soviet Union and its endeavor to cement the communist party-state system has been manifest all through these years. The Czechoslovak Communist Party continued to support the Soviet plans for a world conference of communist and worker parties, with the view of laying down the binding principles of communist policy in the Sino-Soviet conflict. It backed the initiative of Nikita Khrushchev in 1964, and it seconded a similar project when it was presented, at the turn of 1966, by Khrushchev's successors. On the whole, communist Czechoslovakia continued, also in the second half of the sixties, to favor an integrated communist party-state system, with the Soviet Union in a commanding role. The partisans of a more independent Czechoslovak foreign policy had to wait for a change in the Party leadership.

6: HOPEFUL EXPERIMENT

The Party old guard grouped around Antonín Novotný watched the ferment among the intellectuals in the late sixties with particular mistrust. It had two good reasons for doing so. The experience of Poland and Hungary in 1956, where the artists and the writers had been pioneers of the anti-Stalinist revolt, was not forgotten; besides, engagement in politics has been for generations a strong tradition among the Czech and Slovak intelligentsia. However, Novotný and his men did not seem to have any clear strategy as how to meet this danger. Their moves lacked consistency—they were neither clever nor hard enough. The difficulty in containing the revisionist movement of the Czech and Slovak educated classes primarily rested in the fact that it was not an isolated phenomenon. The recalcitrant intellectuals did but reflect and express the general dissatisfaction of all the élites in the society—economists, industrial managers, scientists—as well as that of the noncommunist population. But the opposition of intellectuals was more conspicuous because they had the opportunity and the skill to formulate their ideas and make them public through mass media. They were not the source of the conflict but rather its first-line protagonists.

An Attempt at Showdown

The team in control acted as if it were not aware of the true nature of this tension. Sporadic and incoherent repressive measures, such as stopping the publication of this or that periodical, purges of editorial boards, and tough censorship brought only the disobedient intellectuals closer to the other social groups who sympathized with them. At the beginning of 1967, a new law introduced special controls of the press which were to prevent the publication of articles and books "detrimental to the interests of the state."[1] The "interests of the state" were defined in a deliberately vague form, in order to deter the editors-in-chief from appraising too leniently the contributions of their staffs; in the terms of the new law, they carried full responsibility for what was printed. However, despite this legislative reform, the unrest "on the cultural front" did not subside in any significant measure.

On the whole, the year 1967 proved to be a crucial period in the confrontation between the Party and the intellectuals. The most important event, from this point of view, was the Fourth Congress of the Union of Czechoslovak Writers in Prague, at the end of June. This Congress provided several leading "revisionist" authors with a platform for voicing merciless criticism of the existing political and economic order. The speakers called for far-reaching reforms and for institutional guarantees of basic human freedoms. They also reminded their audiences of the great national traditions, especially of the First Republic and its leaders, in the first place of Thomas G. Masaryk. Some

---

[1] Cf. Law No. 81, *Sbírka zákonů a nařízení Československé socialistické republiky* ("Collected Laws of the Czechoslovak Socialist Republic), Part 36, Prague, Nov. 8, 1966.

110

condemned the position which the Czechoslovak government had taken, a few weeks earlier, on the Middle East conflict. None of these statements were allowed to appear in the press, but the protests against the unreserved endorsement of the Soviet pro-Arab policies took a dramatic form with the gesture of Ladislav Mňačko, at one time a favorite of the Party leaders, who went into voluntary exile in Israel, in early August.[2]

The group in command in the Communist Party had little choice but to respond to this challenge. First of all, it decided to issue a serious warning to all intellectuals who might be tempted to follow the example of their colleagues who had spoken up at the Fourth Congress. A trial which had been pending for a long time against two Czech artists accused of "providing information on State secrets to the enemy" was speedily staged in Prague. Although the interpretation of the incriminating deed as a "betrayal of a State secret" was positively far-fetched—the defendants helped to publish in the West a Communist Party report on the violations of socialist legal procedures in Czechoslovakia during the Stalinist era of the personality cult—the sentences meted out at the trial were very stiff.[3] Yet the trial, as a deterrent, did not seem to have much effect. Czechoslovak writers and journalists kept on publishing critical articles about the conditions in their country, in the Western press.[4]

[2] Cf. "Mňačko protestiert: Ich gehe nach Israel" ("Mňačko Protests: I am Going to Israel"), *Frankfurter Allgemeine Zeitung*, Aug. 11, 1967.

[3] The document in question was published in Paris, by "Editions Svědectví," under the title *Jménem republiky!* ("In the name of the Republic"), in 1966.

[4] For example, even after the sentencing of the defendants in the Prague trial in July, 1967, two articles by Ludvík Vaculík

Antonín Novotný and his followers understood that the situation called for more drastic measures. At the meeting of the Central Committee of the CPCS, at the end of September, a general counter-attack was launched against the nonconformist writers. Jiří Hendrych, head of the Central Committee's Ideological and Cultural Section, stated that "some members of the Writers' Union were not able to overcome in a correct Marxist way the consequences of the criticism applied to the personality cult, nor could they adopt a correct attitude to our present economic difficulties and to the crisis in the world communist movement..." "Instead," Mr. Hendrych continued, "they succumbed to the ideological offensive of the Western diversionists."[5] On the recommendation of Mr. Hendrych, the Central Committee imposed disciplinary sanctions against all writers who had criticized the leadership at the Fourth Congress; they were either expelled or suspended from the Party. A hard blow was dealt to the Writers' Union itself. It lost its press organ, *Literární noviny* ("Literary News"), which was put under the direct supervision of the Ministry of Information. Further stern punishments were contemplated by the Central Committee, among them the transfer of the Literary Fund, the main source of the Union's income, into the State coffers and the disbanding of the Union's central governing body, the Central Committee, so that the or-

---

appeared in the Swiss weekly *Die Weltwoche* (Zurich), July 21, 1967 and Nov. 24, 1967); on Sept. 3, 1967, a "Manifesto of Czechoslovak Writers" was printed in London by the *Sunday Telegraph*. It criticized bitterly the censorship and interference of the authorities with the cultural life in Czechoslovakia; its author, Ivan Pfaff, was arrested in Nov., 1967, but released in the spring of 1968.

[5] *Rudé právo* (Prague), Sept. 30, 1967.

ganization of the Czechoslovak writers would cease to exist on the national level and would disintegrate into a number of regional centers which could be controlled more easily by the local Party organizations. It is difficult to tell with certainty how much support these proposals could secure among the individual members of the Party's supreme organ. The reports on the discussions during this meeting of the Central Committee, published in the daily press, were extremely brief and scanty. The only fact which the public learned was that the Party had reserved the right to take measures toward the ideological consolidation of Czechoslovak culture.

Yet the reprisals which were carried out, harsh as they may have seemed, lacked consistency. The purged writers were allowed to polemize with the official line in the press. Moreover, the new officials of the Union whom the Party imposed in place of the suspended ones proved to be far from dogmatic dichards; many of them sympathized quite openly with their expelled fellow-members. It was clear that the First Secretary was not able to rally sufficient backing for his plan to crush the intellectual revolt. At most, he could hope for a compromise.

The Boomerang

In reality, the attack leveled by the Party leadership on the "cultural front" failed completely and became a boomerang which precipitated the fall of Antonín Novotný. As early as in September, 1967, at a meeting of the Central Committee, it was evident that the conflict with the intelligentsia was only one aspect of a deep crisis within the whole communist movement. It was not an accident that, after having announced puni-

113

tive sanctions against the nonconformist writers, the Party's governing body had to deal with difficult problems of the national economy. The exchange of opinions was unusually frank, almost stormy. The advocates of the economic reform attacked the leadership as responsible for its slow implementation. They pointed out that the leading group hampered the indispensable renewal of technical executive personnel in industry and in planning while it opposed the dismissal of incompetent directors and managers who held their jobs solely because of their Party allegiance. There was little doubt that the New Economic Model had brought only very modest improvements during the first nine months of its application. The Central Committee in its majority espoused this view but it did not take any action. The matter was referred to the following meeting, scheduled for December, 1967.

By December, the partisans of an unrestricted application of economic reforms realized that their aim could never be achieved with Antonín Novotný in control. The First Secretary would under no circumstances part with his grass-roots organizers whom he had carefully selected and established in their positions and who constituted the backbone of his power. The economic reformers joined forces with those who criticized Novotný on other grounds—because of his anti-intellectual policies, his stalling on the question of rehabilitation of victims of political trials, etc. Their immediate end was to achieve the separation of the two highest functions, that of the First Party Secretary and that of the President of the Republic, hitherto united in the person of Antonín Novotný. It was understood that Novotný would have to relinquish the office of the First Secretary and remain as the head of the State only, possibly until the next presidential elections, slated for

1969. However, Novotný was not willing to accept this solution. Hoping for unreserved support from the Soviet side, he invited the CPSU leader Leonid Brezhnev to the Central Committee meeting, without having previously informed the Committee's members. This maneuver failed. Brezhnev—probably seeing that Novotný was facing a very strong opposition—refused to take sides and gave the First Secretary of the CPCS only very lukewarm support. Novotný discovered that the relation between the Soviet Party and the parties in other communist party states has changed since the time when he had come to power. Yet he put up a tough resistance, backed by about half of the Party Presidium, so that the final decision about his fate had to be postponed to the next session held in January, 1968.

Novotný himself had no illusions about the "gentlemen's agreement" which was offered to him in the form of separation of the two top functions. He knew that it was meant as the first stage of his complete removal from power. That was why he made the last desperate attempt to intimidate his opponents by a show of force. His followers among the military prepared the march of an armored division on Prague, January 4, 1968. This move also failed, reportedly because the majority of the army staff was reluctant to become involved in internal Party struggles.[6] Exposed to relentless attacks from his opponents and abandoned by the Kremlin, Novotný was voted out of the function of First Secretary on January 5, 1968. He was succeeded by Alexander Dubček, a Slovak, member of the Party

[6] Cf. the interview with Major General Egyd Pepich in *Obrana lidu* (Prague), Feb. 24, 1968; cf. also the declaration by the Minister of Defense, Martin Dzúr, in *Rolnicke noviny* (Bratislava), April 4, 1968.

Presidium, a communist with an impeccable Moscow background, the son of an old-time Party member, and a man educated in the Soviet Union.

The fall of Novotný was a signal success for the "revisionist" group. This group left nobody in doubt about its intention to carry out thorough reforms in both the political life and economy. A proof that the "progressives" meant business was given by a sudden suspension of preventive censorship, announced by the Party Presidium on February 6, 1968. The Czechoslovak press and other mass information media took immediate advantage of this measure. Overnight, freedom of expression, such as the Czechs and Slovaks had not experienced for twenty years, was restored. The new lively interest of the public in the printed and broadcast word was further increased by the promise of the leadership to rehabilitate all victims of the Stalinist terror, whose cases could now be openly discussed, and the freedom of the press became an independent factor in bringing about general change.

It is probable, however, that the events in Czechoslovakia would have taken a much slower course had not an accident helped to speed up the development. On February 25, it became known that the chief political officer of the Czechoslovak Army, Lt. General Jan Šejna, a protégé of Antonín Novotný, had escaped to the West and asked for asylum in Washington. The real background of this affair has not yet been explained, but it was known that Šejna was among the staff officers who had recommended a miiitary intervention in favor of Antonín Novotný on the eve of the Central Committee's session in January. It is also suspected that he might have been warned by the circles around the President of the Republic about the investigation which was pending and thus given the chance to escape. The Šejna affair thwarted the hopes of Antonín Novotný and his followers that a counter-attack against the revisionist leadership could be waged soon with the highest office in the State as an operational basis. The situation of President Novotný, who was the former First Secretary, and of several key functionaries in the Party and in the government became precarious. The press, the radio, the television, and numerous mass meetings all over the country called for their resignation. After the removal of the Ministers of Interior and Defense and of the head of the Security Department of the Party, Novotný resigned from the function of the President of the Republic on March 22, 1968. He was succeeded by a retired army general Ludvík Svoboda, an officer of the Czechoslovak Legions in Russia during World War I and the commander-in-chief of the Czechoslovak forces in the Soviet Union during World War II.

The Action Program

As he stepped down from his presidential office, Novotný set in motion a wave of resignations from the top and medium Party ranks. The "liberalization" movement thus gained a new momentum. At the meeting of the Central Committee on March 28–April 5, Novotný and his friends were expelled from the Party Presidium. The main task of this meeting, however, was the adoption of the Action Program of the Communist Party of Czechoslovakia which established the immediate and the medium-range goals of the new leadership. This document faithfully reflected what were the reformers' general concepts and showed clearly where the limits of the intended "democratization" were to be set.

As a whole, the published text of the Action Program confirmed the promises which the representatives of the new course had been giving since the January meeting of the Central Committee. It calls for the restoring of freedom of expression through the abolition of preventive censorship; the freedom of the information may be limited only as far as data important for the defense of the State are concerned. The freedom of assembly is to be guaranteed, to facilitate the creation of voluntary organizations "without any bureaucratic impediments." The right to travel abroad and to stay there, even permanently, must be assured to every citizen. Personal and private property are to be protected, especially from arbitrary interference by the State agencies who are not to enjoy privileged position in any court proceedings. A systematic rehabilitation of all people who have been wronged during the past twenty years is to be carried out. The security apparatus is to be reorganized so that the domain of State Security will be limited to cases of intelligence and foreign espionage. "Every citizen who knows that he did not perpetrate any such act must also know with certainty that neither his opinions and views, nor his religious creed, nor his activity may become subject of the investigation by the State Security."[7] The Action Program also pledges the Party to restore fully the independence of courts, with a clear separation of investigation, prosecution, and trial procedures.

The section devoted to economy is another vital part

[7] See "Akční program Komunistické strany Československa, přijatý na plenárním zasedání ÚV KSČ dne 5, dubna 1968" ("The Action Program of the Communist Party of Czechoslovakia, approved at the plenary session of the Central Committee of the CPCS, April 5, 1968"), as reprinted in *Rudé právo* (Prague), April 10, 1968.

of the Action Program. The new leadership stresses its determination to follow the New Economic Model in its original, unrestricted form, i.e., to effect decentralization in production and planning, to increase the responsibilities of local management, and to introduce wages and premiums based on profit. The personnel holding key technical and administrative positions as representatives of the Communist Party are to be replaced by truly technical experts. For this purpose, the stipulations according to which higher functions could be entrusted to communists only are to be abolished. A certain number of small businesses, chiefly services (shoe repair shops, laundries, restaurants) are to be returned into private ownership.

The Action Program pays special attention to the problems of Czechoslovak foreign trade, particularly to the adverse balance of payments with countries having freely convertible currencies and to enormous surpluses in inconvertible currencies, mainly with the member countries of the COMECON. The Action Program insists that this situation must be remedied and, while the socialist markets will always remain essential for Czechoslovak export, the trade with the West should be considerably enlarged. However, as the document admits, an expansion of trade with the capitalist world is presently hampered by the low quality of many Czechoslovak products. Czechoslovak goods are not competitive on the international market also because of obsolescent production methods, insufficient capital investment, and inadequate raw materials. Therefore, Czechoslovakia must thoroughly modernize its industrial equipment, import progressive know-how from advanced capitalist countries, and look for new sources of quality raw materials. The disparity between the domestic prices and the prices in the international markets is to

119

be gradually removed, in order to "expose the national economy to the pressure of world supply and demand" and raise the standard of Czechoslovak industrial production. The willingness "to co-operate with all interested countries in the field of credit and of capital investment"—in other words, to accept economic aid also from capitalist states—is stressed.[8]

The question of foreign trade orientation is closely linked to the general question of foreign policy. This part of the Action Program is perhaps the most cautious and the most conservative. Stress is put on "vitally important" relations to other communist party states, with special emphasis on the "indestructible alliance between Czechoslovakia and the Soviet Union." The basic principles of Soviet policy on Germany are endorsed by a call for the recognition of the two German states, but the document also acknowledges "the necessity to support the realistically thinking forces in the German Federal Republic." In addition, it commits Czechoslovakia to making "more independent use of the membership in international organizations, especially in the UNO and its agencies."[9]

As to the relations between the two main ethnic groups and as to the status of Slovakia within the Czechoslovak Socialist Republic, the Action Program announces far-reaching changes. It condemns "grave mistakes and deformations inherent in the present constitutional solution." The "asymmetric model" currently used does not respect the principle of equality between the two peoples. The authors of the Action Program believe that the country must "avail itself of the advantage of socialist federalism" in order to re-

[8] *Ibid.*
[9] *Ibid.*

solve this problem. This can be achieved only by means of a special constitutional law, whereby (a) the Slovak National Council will be set up as a legislative body, with a Cabinet of Ministers for Slovakia as its collegial executive organ; (b) the control of the National Committees as organs of local government in Slovakia will be entrusted to Slovak national organs; (c) the jurisdiction of these organs will be extended so as to comprise budget and economic planning; (d) the central government of Czechoslovakia will be expanded by newly created cabinet posts of Undersecretaries (who will be Slovaks wherever the Ministers will be Czechs, and vice versa), as had been the case in the first governments immediately after 1945; (e) the overruling of Slovak representation in matters concerning Slovakia will be rendered impossible. In addition to these constitutional reforms the Action Program recommends that the principle of equality of both ethnic elements be respected in the personnel policies in the civil service.[10]

The document also envisages a revision of the status of ethnic minorities, in consequence of which also the Germans are to enjoy "a complete and real political, economic, and cultural equality." In comparison with the spirit and letter of the 1960 Constitution, these reforms represent a truly radical change.[11]

However, the most important section of the Action Program by far deals with the future role of the Communist Party. This section has also caused the greatest controversy, in both the discussions within the CPCS and the comments of the leaders and the mass media of the other communist party states. Following reports from reliable sources, the original draft reserved

[10] *Ibid.*
[11] *Ibid.*

for the CPCS "a leading role among other social and political groups." In the final version, the place of the Party in the State was redefined in a rather traditional way, to appear again as tantamount to a monopoly of power.[12] The stress on the leading role of the Communist Party was probably not meant for domestic consumption only; it seems that it should also provide an argument in the dispute with other parties of the system who have been accusing the new Czechoslovak leadership of "abandoning the path of Socialism."

The Post-January Scene

The Action Program was published amidst a great ferment which was stimulated by the fall of the old-guard Party leaders and by the suspension of censorship. An unprecedented wave of interest in public and political life rose among both the Party's rank and file and the rest of the population outside the Party. Even the noncommunist political parties which had led a shadow existence within the framework of the National Front—mainly the Czechoslovak Socialists and the Czechoslovak People's Party—registered a large influx of new members and the circulation of their press increased considerably. Still more active were the different nonpolitical organizations and movements, such as youth, agricultural co-operatives, and trade unions, Everywhere, discredited officials were resigning or were being dismissed from their positions. Often, the members of various organizations refused to stay within old organizational structures and proceeded to form new independent bodies. Groups which had existed before

[12] Cf. *ibid.*

the 1948 coup d'état were reconstituted, for example, the Boy Scout Movement, or the popular national gymnastic organization "Sokol." Significant for the new situation was also the establishment of new noncommunist groups with clearly political interests that could be considered nuclei or substitutes for oppositional parties. The victims of political persecution in the fifties who had been tried under the infamous paragraph 231 of the Penal Code started organizing "Club 231," and an even more thorough attempt to provide nonmembers of existing political parties with a voice in public affairs took form in the "Club of the politically engaged non-Partisans" ["Klub angažovaných nestraníků"—KAN]. Until the early summer of 1968, the legal status of these revived and newly constituted groups and organizations remained somehow equivocal: They were not explicitly forbidden although they were not authorized, either, by the Ministry of Interior.

Many foreign observers feared, in the late spring of 1968, that the pace of liberalization would slow down and the conservatives would gain strength. Instead, the new leadership gained in consolidation. Its orientation could be defined as "left of the center"—if we accept the connotation "left" as identical with "more liberal" or "democratic." There was no comeback for the "dogmatists"; on the contrary, the Stalinist old-guard continued to lose influence.

The plenary meeting of the Central Committee, held from May 29 till June 1, 1968, confirmed this trend. Almost the entire Novotný group was ousted from the supreme body of the CPCS and Novotný himself, along with a number of other former Stalinists, was suspended from Party membership, pending the investigation of their role in the political processes of the "personality-cult era." Another sign of continuing reform was the

123

convocation by the Central Committee of the Fourteenth Party Congress for September 9, 1968, about two years earlier than scheduled. Although the more radical voices called for an extraordinary congress to be held immediately, it could seem, in the spring of 1968, and barring the eventuality of foreign intervention, that the date chosen by the Central Committee served better the cause of "democratization": It was neither so premature as to carry the risk of arresting the reform process at a too early stage, nor was it so remote as to permit the "liberalization" momentum to dissipate and the "conservative" forces to rally for a counteroffensive.

The Central Committee also dealt with the problem of Czecho-Slovak relations. It called for a government commission to prepare in the Czech provinces of Bohemia and Moravia the constitution of administrative and legislative bodies corresponding to those already existing in Slovakia. This step toward a federal organization of the state was considered necessary by the Central Committee also for psychological reasons: It was supposed to awaken the Czech population to the knowledge that a federalist solution would be in harmony not only with the Slovak but also with the Czech ethnic interests. The supreme Party organ thus reacted to the frequent complaint among the Slovak communists that there was little enthusiasm among the Czechs for a constitutional reform along federalist lines—an attitude hardly surprising with the ethnic group that has always represented a solid majority in the country and has never had any reason to consider its national identity threatened. In order to give a good example, the Central Committee ruled that the federalist organizational pattern should be also applied to the Communist Party, with special Czech governing bodies set up in Bohemia and Moravia. It was interesting to note that the resolution repeatedly used the term "Czech provinces" although the Constitution of 1960 had abolished Bohemia and Moravia as political and administrative units.[13]

Equally important documents, voted as the issue of the Central Committee Meeting in June, 1968, were the "Resolution Concerning the Current Situation and Further Action to Be Taken by the Party" and the "Proclamation of the Central Committee to the Party Members and All People." These summed up the basic goals of the Action Program, reiterated the promise to restore and respect the human and civil rights, and pledged the Communist Party to a closer and more intensive co-operation with its partners in the National Front, so that "all forces which are standing on the basis of the socialist order could participate in the building of an advanced socialist society and thus have their share in the administration of the state and in the political power." However, these resolutions refuted in quite unequivocal terms the idea of an independent opposition party.[14]

Striking in both documents was the insistence upon the "strictly internal character of the Czechoslovak process of change" and the necessity for other countries "not to interfere with this process." The "Resolution Concerning the Current Situation" stressed, also that "Czechoslovakia's relations with the Soviet Union, other socialist countries, and the international communist movement are based on the principle of internationalism and full respect for specific conditions of each nation." The "Proclamation to the Party Mem-

[13] Cf. *Rudé právo* (Prague), June 3, 1968.
[14] Cf. *Rudé právo* (Prague), June 2, 1968.

bers and to All People," on the other hand, promised to "bring more initiative of our own into Czechoslovak foreign policy."[15] The frequency of these references was far from accidental and could be understood only in view of the attitude of the neighboring communist party states and their reactions to what has been happening in Czechoslovakia since the "historical" date of January 5, 1968.

[15] Cf. *ibid.*

7: SOVIET INTERVENTION AND ITS AFTERMATH

While the previous waves of de-Stalinization had been largely inspired by the Soviet example, the "democratization" process that began in Czechoslovakia in January, 1968, was rather obstructed and complicated by the country's affiliation with the communist party-state system. This thaw had its own momentum, independent of the general trends of development in Central and Eastern Europe. The events in Czechoslovakia caught most communist parties and governments abroad unprepared. Official information media of these countries took a long time before they decided on a definite line of interpretation.

Also, the reaction of the press, radio, and television varied from country to country and was shaded according to the stage of emancipation from the Soviet control which this or that state among the party states had reached. The quickest and the most sympathetic response to the "new Czechoslovak road" came from Yugoslavia. A relatively early and positive reaction could be observed in Rumania, though there the coverage was selective, underscoring the facts which pointed to the will of the new Czechoslovak leadership to pursue a more independent foreign policy. The January plenum elicited a cautious, though not unsympathetic, response in Hungary. Polish media, after initial hesitation, started to bring more extensive news about Czechoslovakia but abstained from any comment for a considerable length of time. The slowest to report this news were the Soviet, Bulgarian, and East German mass media. Albanian and Chinese press and radio took a clearly negative attitude right from the beginning.

Response to Czechoslovak Reforms Among the Communist Party States

As events moved on and neither silence nor scanty coverage could any longer substitute for a policy, individual states' attitudes within the communist party-state system became more pronounced. For Czechoslovakia, the position taken by her immediate neighbors was of greatest consequence. On the whole, it was not very favorable. It seemed as if Czechoslovakia which once had been considered part of the "Iron Triangle" along with Poland and East Germany had to face another triangle—East Germany, Poland, and the Soviet Union—forged by the wish to contain and neutralize the international impact of the Czechoslovak reform movement. Every one of these three neighbors had its own specific reasons to fear the new development in Czechoslovakia: the Soviet Union, because of possible loss of a vital outpost in Central Europe; East Germany, because of an eventual uncovering of its southern flank and because of a feeling of insecurity, natural to a regime which even after a quarter of a century had not been able to take firm root in the population; and Poland, because the democratization in Czechoslovakia coincided with a contrary trend in Polish domestic politics.

128

The most adversely critical stand on the events in Czechoslovakia was taken by East German politicians and journalists. Their comments provoked two diplomatic protests from Prague by the end of spring. The Polish government protested in Czechoslovakia, on May 5, 1968, against what it had termed as "unfriendly reporting in the Czechoslovak press on the events in Poland." Also the Soviets complained through diplomatic channels about two specific articles in two Czech noncommunist dailies which had hinted at Soviet complicity in the political trials of the fifties and in the recent Šejna affair.[1]

The official hostility of these three countries to the Czechoslovak "democratization" experiment did not remain restricted to polemics in the press and to diplomatic protests, but was transferred soon to government and Party circles. On a very short notice, a meeting was convened in Dresden in East Germany on March 23, 1968, where top representatives of the U.S.S.R., East Germany, Poland, Hungary, Bulgaria, and Czechoslovakia reportedly discussed "urgent questions of common interest." Significantly enough, Rumania did not participate in this session. The circumstance that the meeting was called less than twenty-four hours after the resignation of Antonín Novotný from the presidency of the Republic left hardly any doubt as to the nature of these questions of common interest. The anxiety felt by the U.S.S.R. and its allies over the Czechoslovak problem appears even more obvious if we take into consideration that the Dresden talks followed shortly after a meeting of the Warsaw Treaty Organization in Sofia, that gave the delegates an ample opportunity to

---

[1] Cf. ČETEKA (Czechoslovak Press Agency) release, June 12, 1968.

examine any problem of mutual interest known at that time. The choice of the place, too, was significant: It pointed to the fact that the initiative came from East Berlin. No details about the dealings in the capital of Saxony have been made public, but some Czechoslovak participants confirmed later that the democratization process in Czechoslovakia had been the main item on the agenda. They assured the public that the Czechoslovak representatives "had succeeded in convincing their friends and allies that the present changes meant in no way a departure from the path of Socialism."[2]

It is difficult to believe that all doubts were dispelled in Dresden. The developments in Czechoslovakia remained a subject of paramount interest in the communist party-state system for many months to come. Meetings and visits of top communist officials in consequence of these developments followed one another. On May 4, 1968, the First Secretary of the CPCS Dubček and Prime Minister Černík traveled to Moscow for "consultations on pending problems." It seems that this State visit did not succeed in appeasing mistrust and apprehension, because, immediately after the departure of the Czechoslovak leaders from the Kremlin, a new summit meeting of the representatives of the Warsaw Pact countries was called in Moscow—this time excluding not only Rumania but also Czechoslovakia. The official sources maintained an even stricter silence on these talks than on the consultations in Dresden; yet it did leak out that the East German and Polish delegations had pressed for an energetic collective action against the revisionist group in Prague, while the Hungarian communist leader János Kádár had recommended moderation. The movements of troops in southern Poland and along the border between Czecho-

[2] Cf. *Rudé právo* (Prague), March 25, 1968.

slovakia and Eastern Germany, reported at the same time, made the situation appear rather dramatic. However, there was no intervention, military or political, nor were there economic sanctions applied against Czechoslovakia by the U.S.S.R. and her allies.

The arrival of a Soviet army delegation in Czechoslovakia in May, 1968, moved some commentators to speculations about possible Soviet pressure for permanent quartering of military units of the Warsaw Treaty Organization in Czechoslovakia. Top Czechoslovak officials categorically denied such possibility.[3] Late in June, an exercise of the Warsaw Pact staff units took place in Czechoslovakia, which provoked a certain uneasiness among the population. However, until early summer, 1968, there were no signs that these or other units would remain permanently in the country.

Informed observers ascribed more importance to the visit of Alexei Kosygin, which took place about the same time. During his stay in Czechoslovakia, which was officially presented as a private trip for a cure at Karlsbad, Kosygin had several meetings with leaders of the Czechoslovak Party. It is generally believed that these meetings helped to stabilize the explosive situation which had existed before. On the other hand, the new Czechoslovak Party leadership had been avoiding, more carefully than ever, anything which might suggest any drastic change in the orientation of Czechoslovak foreign policy. It went so far as to declare the establishment of diplomatic relations with the Federal Republic of Germany to be "a long term goal" and the renewal of relations with Israel "inopportune."[4] Concerning the planned conference of world communist parties—a project particularly important in the eyes of

[3] Radio Prague, May 22, 1968.
[4] Cf. the declaration of the Czechoslovak Minister of Foreign Affairs, Jiří Hájek, as carried by Radio Prague, June 12, 1968.

Soviet politicians—the Czechoslovak Communist Party continued to support the U.S.S.R. It gave proof of its loyalty both at the first and at the second preparatory conferences in Budapest, in February and in April, 1968, by voting for the Soviet proposals.

Pressure and hostility were then not the only reaction to the Czechoslovak "democratization" from the countries of the communist party-state system; there has been also active support. While the Hungarian official media clearly stated on several occasions that Hungary was "watching Czechoslovakia's efforts with good-will and approval,"[5] Rumania and Yugoslavia went farther and gave the new Czechoslovak group in control an open diplomatic and political backing. In a joint communiqué signed at the close of the visit of Nicolae Ceausescu, the First Secretary of the Rumanian Communist Party, in Belgrade, on June 1, 1968, the Rumanian leader and his host, President Tito, condemned "the pressures, threats, and interference in the affairs of other states" and stressed "the exclusive right of each Party to independently fashion its policy in building socialism in its own country."[6] Thus the events in Czechoslovakia not only exposed radical differences of opinions among the communist nations but also contributed to the creation of new ideological and political alliances within the communist party-state system.

The Dialogue of the Deaf

Meanwhile, the behind-the-scene struggle of conflicting views on how to handle the situation in Czecho-

[5] Cf. *Nepszabadsag* (Budapest), June 4, 1968.
[6] Cf. the joint communiqué issued in Belgrade on June 1st, 1968, as carried by the Yugoslav press agency TANJUG.

slovakia went on among and within the leaderships of the Soviet Union and other communist party states. In July, 1968, a new summit conference was called in Warsaw, to which the Czechoslovak Communist Party was invited but did not send any delegation; while it expressed its willingness to discuss "any questions of mutual interest" on a bilateral basis, it refused to "sit on the defendant's bench of an international tribunal."[7] Details of what happened at this conference are not known, as it was held in absolute secrecy. However, it seems that it was there that the opinion about the necessity of a military intervention prevailed and that partisans of a hard course finally succeeded in making their views acceptable. The final communiqué, issued on July 17, 1968, and a joint letter of the five communist parties (Rumania abstained, as usual, from the conference) to the Communist Party of Czechoslovakia would suggest such an impression. The situation in the Czechoslovak Socialist Republic was described as extremely critical, in an obvious intent to justify eventual drastic action. In unmistakable terms, the Warsaw meeting participants claimed the right "to come to help a fraternal working people in any socialist country" where the bases of the socialist order are threatened.[8]

On the other hand, it is very likely that an exact date for intervention was not fixed—and maybe even not discussed—in Warsaw, although it must have been clear to the advocates of this solution that military

[7] *Práce* (Prague), July 11, 1968.

[8] Cf. the text of the letter of the representatives of the five CPs, dated July 17, 1968, as released by the Hungarian press agency MTI and reprinted by all dailies of all party states participating in the Warsaw talks as well as by the Czechoslovak mass media, July 18, 1968.

action was becoming more and more risky as time was passing by. If not carried out before the Fourteenth Congress of the Czechoslovak Party, slated for September 9, the operation might have lost its formally legal basis, tenuous as it was. Technically, of course, it did not present much difficulty: the necessary military contingents had been kept in combat readiness for many weeks in all neighboring party states and the regular Warsaw Pact maneuvers, held in Czechoslovakia at the end of June and the beginning of July, 1968, had provided an excellent opportunity to test their mobility. The move itself could be effected according to the strategic plans of the communist alliance worked out against the threat of possible invasion of Czechoslovakia from the West.

Psychologically, the conference at Warsaw and the letter of the five "fraternal parties" achieved the very opposite of what they were expected to achieve. Instead of intimidating the Czechoslovak reform movement, they gave it a new impulse and rallied behind it those strata of the population which hitherto had remained passive. If the opponents of the Czechoslovak "liberalization" had aimed to reverse the trend of the CPCS toward a more independent course closer to the nation's interests, it was too late for *any* kind of action after the Warsaw meeting. Not even the most conservative individuals, unless they were willing to accept the stigma of quislings, could ignore the force of national unity. Public reaction to the letter of the five allies forced the Communist Party of Czechoslovakia to adopt a firm, uncompromising stand. It was a rare spectacle: For the first time in some twenty-five years, a spontaneous movement, spread from the grassroots organizations, was respected by the leadership; similarly, the leadership tasted the exultation of having the support of the people.

The CPCS replied to the Warsaw conference participants that there was no immediate danger of any counterrevolution in Czechoslovakia. It pointed out that no
measures had ever been taken by the Czechoslovak
government, either in domestic or foreign politics,
which could be interpreted as a retreat from the principles of socialism or as an attempt to defect from the
communist alliance. The Czechoslovak party presidium
refused to accept the collective condemnation of its
Warsaw Pact partners but reiterated its willingness to
discuss problems of mutual concern with any one of
them in bilateral talks.[9] It was characteristic of the climate then prevailing in Czechoslovakia, as compared to
the conditions in the neighboring communist countries,
that the Czech and Slovak press and other mass media
gave full publicity to the letter of the Five, while the
mass media of the party states represented in Warsaw
did not carry the Czechoslovak reply at all, or only in
an arbitrarily restricted and distorted form. In these
countries a mood was obviously being built up to favor
an eventual "fraternal help to the Czechoslovak proletariat in distress." The engineers of these plans did not
refrain even from such transparent fabrications as,
for example, planting a load of old American firearms,
dating from World War II, in a place in Bohemia where
it was later found by "vigilant, faithful Leninist members of the Czechoslovak Communist Party," as the
East German press claimed; a commission of the Czechoslovak Ministry of Interior exposed this incident as a
provocation.

The offer of the Czechoslovak party leaders to con-

[9] Cf. the declaration of the Plenum of the Czechoslovak Com-
munist Party, enlarged by the delegates elected to the 14th
Congress, of July 19, 1968, as published in "Rudé právo,"
Prague, July 20, 1968.

duct bilateral negotiations was, on the other hand, accepted by their opposite numbers in Central and Eastern Europe and, indeed, a new exchange of opinion took place during the last days of July and the first days of August, 1968. Although few details are known about these talks, it can be assumed that they reconfirmed, on the whole, the spectrum of differences among the Warsaw Pact members. The differences ranged from the rigid and irreconcilable stand of the German Democratic Republic to a very apparent readiness to compromise of János Kádár's Hungary. However, by far the most important negotiations took place between the delegation of the CPSU and that of the CPCS, at the Soviet-Czechoslovak border in Cierna nad Tisou, from July 29 through August 1, 1968. Exact contents of these talks were not made public, to the great dismay of Czechoslovak journalists who had, shortly before, obtained a promise from the Party and the government that no "secret diplomacy" would ever be conducted on party or state level. There can be no doubt that two almost diametrically opposed points of view were confronted at this occasion. Criticism of Czechoslovak developments, as presented by the Soviets, can be reconstructed from the numerous comments which then appeared in the press. It seems that the two partners disagreed not only in the valuation of the trends of the Czechoslovak reform movement—the hosts being calm and confident, the guests alarmed about a possible danger of counterrevolution—but also in their general conceptions of Socialism, socialist democracy, proletarian internationalism, and socialist economy. It was this complete incompatibility of the basic criteria that made an accommodation impossible and, in spite of a dramatic change in the Soviet-Czechoslovak relationship brought about by the subsequent events, obstructed any pragmatic, realistic compromise or even any useful dialogue between the two countries.

The main recurrent Soviet objection to the situation in Czechoslovakia was that the Czechoslovak communists "neglected the principle of the leading role of the Party in a Socialist state." It would have been extremely hard for the Soviet critics to illustrate their charge on a concrete example. On the contrary, the argument of the Czechoslovak communists that not a single step had been taken, *on the institutional level*, which could justify the assumption that the Party was giving up its monopoly of power, appeared irrefutable. Another criticism was that the Czechoslovak leaders tolerated a "weakening of the ties between Czechoslovakia and the other countries of the Socialist camp." Here again, the position of the Czechoslovak Party seemed to be very strong. The Party never took, nor ever contemplated taking, any measures *on the international relations level* which resulted either in diminishing the contractual obligations toward the members of the communist party-state system or in increasing commitments toward the nations outside this system. The third most frequently formulated charge was that the Czechoslovak reform program encouraged and invited "anti-Socialist views and ideas." In an objective discussion, it would have been easy for the accused Czechoslovak leadership to embarrass their interlocutors by challenging them to point out a practical example of such mistakes, for an open condemnation of socialism had never appeared in any Czech newspaper or in any radio or television program, not even when the freedom of the press was at the highest, in the summer of 1968. However, it was apparent that none of these arguments would carry much weight with the Soviet representatives; two completely different philosophies were clashing here. While the Czechoslovak communists, party officials and intellectuals alike, tended to interpret the notions of "leading role of the Party," "co-operation and solidarity with the peoples of the World Socialist System," and "inviolability of the socialist order in Czechoslovakia" rather in their literal sense, the Soviet party politicians continued to understand them in terms of absolute power which did not differ significantly from those valid during the previous era of "personality cult." Soviet communists did not view these concepts so much as a set of explicit rules and clearly defined institutions, the observance of which can be proved and measured by objective criteria, but rather as a climate or an all-pervasive mood which should prevail in every party state. Thus the "leading role of the Party" appeared to them not as *a duty to lead*, but as *a license to monopolize* all political activity; not to be *the first among many*, but to be *the only one*; and not *to stimulate*, but *to permeate and control* the entire public life. Also the "international proletarian solidarity" did not mean to the Soviets the obligation to co-operate with the rest of the communist party-state system, but rather the duty to subscribe without reserve to the foreign policy line laid down by the Soviet Union. The "anti-socialist views" which the Czechoslovak Communist Party was rendering itself guilty of tolerating were, in the perspective of the Kremlin policy-makers, all views which were not in concordance with the orthodox Soviet communist doctrine.

It was reported from Cierna that, when Alexander Dubček argued that his reformist policies had full support of the whole nation—he could even produce a declaration of solidarity with no less than four million signatures—the CPSU chief Brezhnev retorted: "This only proves that your party has abandoned its leading role." Hardly anything would illustrate better the gap between the two concepts of socialist government; the turn from the dictatorship of the proletariat to the "state of all people" has still remained heresy in the eyes of the Soviet ideologists. It seems that the talks at Cierna, far from settling the dispute, deepened further the disagreement between the partners—as, on the whole, did every confrontation of the Czechoslovak communists with their comrades from most of the communist party states. The same can be said about the subsequent meeting in Bratislava, on August 3, 1968, where again representatives of all five countries were present. Nevertheless, the final communiqué from this conference, which summed up the results of negotiations both at Cierna and in Bratislava, gave the impression that the allies had been satisfied with the outcome and had resigned themselves to a workable compromise.[10] Many renowned observers interpreted this as a triumph for the Czechoslovak leadership and praised Alexander Dubček for not having overplayed his triumph and having "permitted the Big Brother to save his face."

The Invasion

In the night of August 20 to August 21, 1968, more than half a million troops of the Warsaw Pact

---

[10] See the final communique of the Bratislava Conference, as recorded in *Izvestia* (Moscow), Aug. 4, 1968; cf. further the comment on the Cierna and Bratislava talks in *Pravda* (Moscow), Aug. 5 and Aug. 6, 1968; in *Literaturnaja Gazeta* (Moscow), Aug. 14, 1968; and—particularly—the editorial by Yuri Zhukov in *Pravda* (Moscow), Aug. 16, 1968.

countries, with the exception of Rumania, invaded Czechoslovak territory. Only a historian who will have gained access to first-hand sources of information will be able to tell with certainty whether the feeling of relief, prevailing after the talks at Bratislava, was justified or not—that is, whether the Soviets actually had meant to give the Czechoslovak experiment a chance and changed their mind only later, or whether all negotiations from the very beginning had been a smoke screen and a treacherous game. It is easy to bring proofs in support of the opinion that the intervention had been planned since early spring 1968. The most convincing evidence would be the preparedness of the Soviet and allied troops, their incessant movements along Czechoslovak borders, as well as reluctance of some of them to evacuate Czechoslovakia after the summer military exercise. However, the alertness of the Warsaw-Pact armies might not have signified more than that the intervention had been considered as one serious *alternative* among several, with different courses kept open. On the other hand, it would not be difficult to argue that the invasion must have been opted for on the spur of a moment—or, at least, that the actual order to the troops to move into Czechoslovakia was given on very short notice, under the influence of some precise event or fact. Many circumstances, in the first place the astoundingly poor preparation of the political, that is, the most important aspect of the intervention, would point in this direction.

If this was actually so, what could have been this definite event that tilted the scales in favor of the invasion? True enough, the political scene in Czechoslovakia remained lively after the talks at Cierna and in Bratislava. The long-postponed state visits of the two protagonists of national independence and sovereignty of the communist party states, Yugoslav President Tito and Rumanian Prime Minister Ceausescu, were at last taking place. The response of the Czechoslovak public to them, especially to that of Marshal Tito, left no doubt what the country felt about the Moscow-style proletarian internationalism. However, it is likely that, far more than a possible resurrection of the Little Entente spirit, it was the internal development which provided the final impulse to the military action. On the assumption that some concrete event did alarm the Soviet leaders to the point when an armed intervention appeared as immediate necessity, it would seem that the formal constitution of the Social Democratic Party—or, more accurately, of its Preparatory Committee—in Prague on August 15, 1968, might have triggered the action. However, on the other hand, the intensive press campaign in the U.S.S.R. and other Warsaw Pact countries immediately before the invasion which was an obvious propaganda build-up, paid little attention to this apparently significant fact. Another theory has it that, during a series of bilateral talks with the representatives of the smaller party states, such differences of opinion came up between the Czechoslovak communists and their comrades that these latter put whatever more pressure was necessary on the Kremlin to move it to intervene. A particularly active role in this connection is ascribed to the Chairman of the State Council of the G.D.R. Walter Ulbricht, who visited Czechoslovakia the week after the conclusion of the Bratislava conference.

Reaction of the Party and the Population

No matter what the most immediate motives for the invasion might have been, the operation earned the re-

141

spect of military experts on both sides of the Iron Curtain as an absolutely faultless strategic move. On the political side, however, the intervention was far from faultless; in fact, the history of world communism has hardly seen a politically more confused operation.

The invading units of the Soviet Union, Poland, East Germany, Hungary, and Bulgaria—in an estimated total number of 600,000—met with no military resistance but with a virtually unanimous passive resistance of the population. This unanimity did not have to bother the invaders any more than the nation-wide resistance of the Hungarian people did in November, 1956, but there were important new elements in the situation. It soon became evident that the occupant had no collaborators to rely upon; from this point of view the resistance was unprecedented. The usual "classical" measures of the Soviets—the arrest of the leaders and the seizure of the mass communications media—revealed themselves ineffective, as there was literally nobody to take the place of the silenced leadership and to put press, radio, and television at the occupant's service. On the contrary, the mass media personnel went underground in an admirably organized manner and, from hiding, continued to voice protests and to spoil the invaders' propaganda. A clandestine Party Congress was called to a Prague factory, where it was camouflaged as a staff meeting; it was held in lieu of the Fourteenth Congress which the invasion now made impossible. The Congress newly endorsed the reform program of the January Plenum, expelled dogmatist members, and expressed its full support for the jailed top officials. The Czechoslovak Trade Union Council proclaimed a general strike which was observed with impressive discipline all over the country. Students and members of youth organizations went into the streets and engaged the invading troops in discussions about the purpose and the justification of the invasion. Wall inscriptions in perfect Russian revealed to the hundreds of thousands of Red Army members the true feelings of the nation; here the twenty years of compulsory instruction in Russian language backfired on those who had imposed them. This picture did not agree with what the troops had heard in their ideological briefings for the operation: They had been told that a handful of counter-revolutionaries and Western agents oppressed the great majority of the Czechoslovak working people, who were anxious for their liberation by their "Soviet brothers."

Yet the most stunning experience for the invaders must have been the impossibility to find a group, however small, which would legalize the invasion by a formal request for "help," even issued *ex post*, and which could provide a basis for a quisling Party leadership and government. The curious fact that the Warsaw Pact armies marched into Czechoslovakia *prior* to the constitution of such a group permits two explanations: Either the Soviets were absolutely sure they would find sufficient response whenever they would come to "aid the imperiled Socialism," or the decision to carry out the operation was taken in such a precipitate way that there simply was no time to set up a new team—as, for instance, had been the case in Hungary, twelve years earlier. If the first surmise is correct, it would be interesting to know on what grounds and from what sources the Kremlin policy-makers gained the impression that the replacement of the reformist leadership would be a problem so easy to solve. Serious doubts about the validity of this theory arise if we ask why the same individuals or groups, who had succeeded in convincing the Soviets about a warm reception of the intervention by the great majority of the working people in Czechoslovakia, did not later co-operate in the Soviet efforts to establish new, Soviet-subservient Party and government organs. It is possible, of course, that these informants had the confidence of the Soviets but neither the popularity nor the record which would qualify them to succeed Alexander Dubček and his associates; such a description would fit, almost perfectly, the former First Party Secretary and the President of the Republic Antonín Novotný, who, all through the eight months of the new course, had been in a close contact with the Soviet Embassy in Prague and its top official, Ambassador Tchervonenko. The possibility cannot be ruled out, either, that the Soviets had obtained a promise of collaboration from certain personalities in the Communist Party of Czechoslovakia, but that these individuals revised their stand after the invasion, under the impression of the unanimity of popular support for the reformist leaders. However, many conservative Party officials later denied explicitly any collusion with the occupationists, before as well as after intervention.

Thus, the theory that, due to a very sudden decision to carry out the military operation, lack of time was responsible for the poor preparation of the invasion's political aspects remains the most probable. In this light, the Kremlin's action would appear to be a momentary alarm reaction of an irresolute and disoriented leadership, shaken by chronic internal dissensions rather than a "diabolic Asiatic ruse." The circumstance, for example, that the proclamation to the "Czech and Slovak working people" that had been waiting for twenty-four hours on the desks of the press agencies in the five party states participating in the invasion had to be finally withdrawn without publication because of the lack of signatures, or the fact that, three days later, the communication media controlled by the occupational forces made public a "Manifesto of Czechoslovak Communists, faithful to the ideas of Marxism-Leninism" but could not put one single name under it, seem to be very convincing indicators of the totally improvised character of the whole action.

Strange Compromise

At the height of the crisis, when the deadlock became patent and the passive resistance of the Czechoslovak population threatened to erupt any moment into a violent confrontation with the occupational forces, the President of the Republic Ludvík Svoboda, one of the few top leaders of the State present in the country and not under arrest, went to Moscow to negotiate a solution with the Soviets. In Prague, his travel to the Soviet capital was presented as an act taken on his own initiative; however, the pomp with which he was received upon his arrival there, showed that his step was most welcome to the Soviets. Maybe the CPSU leadership hoped to make the same easy deal with President Svoboda as Stalin and Gottwald had made with President Beneš in 1948, or Hitler with President Hácha in 1939. Whatever their expectations might have been, the fact remains that the talks proved to be very difficult. After four days of negotiations, the Soviet Party and government leaders agreed to return the interned Czechoslovak politicians to power, in exchange for the promise that the situation in Czechoslovakia would be "normalized." There was little explanation given what was to be understood by "normalization," except that "anti-Socialist elements" were to be "rendered harmless" and anti-Soviet attacks and the criticism of the Soviet move in the Czechoslovak press was to be curbed. Until the satisfaction of this demand, the troops of the Warsaw Pact were to remain in Czechoslovakia. However, it could be guessed from various hints by the Soviet representatives that some contingents of the Red Army would stay in the country even after "normalization" would be achieved, in order to "protect the borders of the Socialist camp from the aggression by West German revanchists."

On August 26, 1968, Alexander Dubček and his group returned to Prague and resumed their offices in the Party and in the government. Though their personal experience must have been a serious shock and though they had to dampen many a naive hope pinned by the population and the Party rank-and-file members on their return, their comeback was an admission of failure by the Soviets. Moscow gave thus to understand that it did not see how Czechoslovakia and the Communist Party there could be led, at least at that time, by a team other than that of the hated "revisionists." This admission was all the more obvious, as hardly forty-eight hours earlier the official organ of the CPSU, "Pravda" of Moscow, had denounced Alexander Dubček as "a traitor to the Czechoslovak proletariat and to the cause of international Communism."[11]

While the internal difficulties encountered in the occupied Czechoslovakia were probably the main motive of the Soviet retreat from the original plan to bring about a sweeping change, international complications ensuing from the invasion might have also played a certain role during the "four-day crisis." The indignation in the free world was great, and all the leading

[11] *Pravda* (Moscow), Aug. 22, 1968.

statesmen of the West condemned the Soviet action. However, judging from Soviet behavior at similar occasions in the past, it is not very likely that the Kremlin policy-makers were much impressed by these reactions. What might have weighed with them more seriously was going on in the framework of the United Nations, during the first days of the intervention. In contrast to what had happened in the wake of the Hungarian revolution in November, 1956, both the permanent Czechoslovak representative to the United Nations and the Czechoslovak Minister of Foreign Affairs denounced the invasion and flatly denied that anyone, either in the government or in the Party, would have ever invited the Warsaw Pact armies to enter Czechoslovakia. The Soviet move was thus deprived of even its most artificial formal basis.

Yet, by far the most effective means of pressure on the international level were probably those applied by several important centers of the world communist movement. The U.S.S.R. was not even able to rally on its side a convincing majority of the communist party states. Among the ruling communist parties outside the five who participated in the intervention, only the CP of North Vietnam approved the move without reservation; the rest voiced a very strong protest or took, at best, an ambiguous stand without hiding the fact that, in their opinion, the Soviet action could not be justified on any legal grounds. Among the parties in the remaining world, the response was even more crushing. The Soviet Union received support from a bare half-dozen of them, mostly negligible sects in the underground, and even these sometimes reached their decision only after serious internal conflicts. The two largest Western components of the international communist movement—the French and Italian communist parties—as well as a majority of the smaller parties, rejected the intervention in quite unmistakable terms. These consequences must have been particularly keenly resented by that part of the Soviet leadership which had been setting hopes on the International Communist Conference, slated for November, 1968, as a step towards greater cohesion of world communism. There is little doubt that the invasion dealt a serious blow to these hopes; some Western observers are even of the opinion that the conflict between Moscow and other communist parties over Czechoslovakia was "a death spasm of international communism."[12]

Another important question is whether the decision to intervene actually put an end to the obvious differences of opinion among the Soviet leaders about the Czechoslovak issue, that had existed before August 21, 1968. It does not seem that it was so; on the contrary, there are signs that the policy of force adopted in this respect continues to meet with little enthusiasm on the part of at least some members of the top organs of the CPSU. It was probably no accident that the Central Committee of the Soviet Party, which had met shortly before the invasion, took another two months to meet again, obviously to endorse the principles of the strange compromise reached with the Czechoslovak representatives after the occupation. No points of agenda were mentioned in the final communiqué of this session, but the unusually emphatic assertion that the policy of the present leaders "enjoys wholesale and unreserved support of all Party members and of all Soviet people" would rather suggest that the team in control was in dire need of such assertions.[13]

[12] Cf. interview with Zbigniew Brzezinski on the NBC radio and television, August 21, 1968, in the evening.

[13] *Pravda* (Moscow), Oct. 22, 1968.

Czechoslovakia after the Invasion

While the intervention of the Warsaw Pact powers in Czechoslovakia created serious new problems for the Soviet Union and further complicated the already rather confused conditions within the world communist movement on the one hand, it rendered, on the other hand, none the less critical the situation of the Czechoslovak Party and the whole regime. However, one circumstance worked in favor of the reformist leaders and made possible what has been ever since considered a minor miracle, namely, their remarkable independent stand on most of the important issues: This was the unanimous support they received from the Czech and Slovak population. The invasion mobilized the last indifferent segments of the nation and virtually closed the gap between the Party members and the noncommunist majority which had paralyzed Czechoslovak political life ever since 1948. It is possible to say that for the first time in twenty years the leadership could claim a general consensus and support. This consensus, of course, was by no means unconditional; it was granted on the assumption that the Communist Party of Czechoslovakia would now represent the will of the people—and this will was to resist the occupation powers. In other words, the concern over maintaining the popular backing drove the communist élites into the opposition to the Soviet Union and the other Warsaw Pact countries who had participated in the intervention. Yet the simple "facts of life" forced the leading team of the CPCS to avoid unnecessary provocations of the invaders, lest new and more drastic foreign interference in domestic matters should occur. In this precarious situation, the Dubček group had to steer an extremely cautious course; the diametrically opposed goals of the U.S.S.R. and of the Czechoslovak people did not leave much room for maneuvering, however subtle and circumspect.

The relations between the Czechoslovak communists and the Soviet leadership in the post-invasion period were marked by uncertainty and mistrust on both sides. The Kremlin, having failed in its first attempt to remove the reformist élite, was anxious to have the invasion and occupation of Czechoslovakia legalized; by returning Dubček and his associates to power it abandoned implicitly the claim that the intervention had taken place on demand of some unspecified "faithful Leninists" in the CPCS. It was obvious that such a legalization could not be sought in the Moscow agreement, signed during the first days of occupation, as this document bore too clear imprints of a dictate. The Czechoslovak leaders carefully avoided everything which might have substantiated the thesis about the Warsaw Pact armies having been "invited" to Czechoslovakia. On the other hand, in view of the unfavorable reaction of the world communist opinion to the invasion, some form of explicit sanction by the Czechoslovak representatives appeared indispensable. After some negotiations, a treaty was signed in Moscow on October 18, 1968, which provided the legal basis, desired by the Soviets, for what is termed in the document "temporary presence of the Soviet troops on the territory of the Czechoslovak Socialist Republic."

The Moscow treaty kept the question of numerical strength of the Soviet occupational units open: it should be "determined by agreement between the governments of the U.S.S.R. and Czechoslovakia."[14] All other troops are to be withdrawn within two months of the

[14] *Rudé Právo* (Prague), Oct. 19, 1968.

date of the ratification of the treaty. Particularly interesting are the provisions of the Article 2, whereby "Soviet troops, their personnel, and members of their families shall observe the legislation in effect in the Czechoslovak Socialist Republic" and "Soviet troops do not interfere in the internal affairs of Czechoslovakia."[15] The degree to which these clauses will be respected by the Soviets will determine the future course of events in Czechoslovakia and the fate of the Dubček political program. The treaty is interesting also from another point of view, commented upon with satisfaction by the CPCS press: It does neither pretend that the Warsaw Pact armies entered the Czechoslovak territory on invitation by the Party or the Government, nor claim that there had been a counterrevolution in Czechoslovakia prior to August 21, 1968.[16]

It seems that the leaders of the CPCS were trying to stress their independence in internal matters. In spite of the fact that they had to carry out certain measures which had been dictated to them by the occupational power (among them the reintroduction of press censorship and the banning of all political groups outside the National Front), they could take the credit of having passed some legislation in accordance with the Party's Action Program of March, 1968, even after the invasion. By far the most important reform thus voted was the new federalist political order, adopted by the National Assembly on October 28, 1968, on the fiftieth anniversary of the foundation of Czechoslovakia.

With this reform coming into force on January 1,

---

[15] Cf. *ibid.*

[16] Alois Svoboda, "Po páteční ratifikaci" ("Following the Ratification on Friday"), in the Party weekly *Politika* (Prague), Oct. 31, 1968.

1969, Czechoslovakia became a federation composed of two members, The Czech Socialist Republic and The Slovak Socialist Republic. Only matters of national concern, such as foreign affairs, defense, and finances, remain now under the authority of the federal government; in all other matters, the executive power is divided between the governments of the two republics. The supreme legislative body, the Federal Parliament, comprises now two houses: The National Assembly and The Chamber of Peoples.[17] Special stipulations about the voting procedure and equal distribution of seats among the two ethnic groups prevent either the Czechs or the Slovaks from being outvoted on issues relating either exclusively or preponderantly to their respective provinces. Also other ethnic elements in Czechoslovakia, including the Germans, obtained full equality in civil rights and guarantees of respect for their ethnic identity.

From the strictly formal point of view, these reforms make inevitable a thorough revision of the Constitution of 1960 which, as we have seen, is very "dogmatic," both in letter and spirit. It will be interesting to see whether such a revision—an indisputably "liberal" move—will be possible in the conditions created by the Soviet intervention. It was characteristic of the situation at the time when the federative principle was enacted that, though this law had been signed by the President of the Republic, no date for the first election into new legislative bodies was set. It would seem that such an election—as, in fact, any election in the period immediately following the occupation—is highly unde-

[17] Literal translation of these Czech terms would be "The Chamber of the People" and "The Chamber of the Nations." However, in Czech and in Slovak, the word "nation" has connotations of the English concept of "ethnic group."

sirable in the eyes of the Soviets, because it could provide an opportunity for the people to demonstrate their true feelings. Whatever the outcome of the vote might be, it would always point to the refusal of the Czechs and the Slovaks to accept the new situation: A spectacular victory of the present Communist Party leadership would have to be interpreted as a manifestation of solidarity with the First Secretary who defied the Soviets, while a defeat of the official ballot or a considerable abstention from the vote would show that majority of citizens reject the present system as a whole. If this assumption is correct, the Soviets, motivated by fear, might obstruct all decisions in all important issues for some time to come, so that the political life in the country could be eventually paralyzed.

On the whole, during the first months after the Soviet intervention, Czechoslovakia presented a picture of undaunted national will and exemplary unity. The degree of intellectual liberty and spiritual independence the Czechs and Slovaks were able to preserve was unprecedented in the history of the communist party-state system. On several occasions, both the people and the élites manifested their dedication to the ideals of democracy and freedom. The most impressive example of this was observed during the celebrations of October 28, which is the Czechoslovak Independence Day, and which in the year of invasion coincided with the fiftieth anniversary of the founding of the Czechoslovak Republic.

The unabated protest mood took new dramatic forms of expression in January, 1969, with the self-immolation of several young people, which deeply shocked the nation and the world. Official representatives of the State and the Party expressed understanding and sympathy with these protesters. Despite the formal reinstating of censorship, the press and other mass media preserved a remarkably frank language and a considerable degree of freedom. It became apparent that the political mobilization, brought about by the forceful Soviet attempt to stop the course of change in Czechoslovakia, would remain an essential feature of the Czechoslovak scene for a long time to come.

Crisis of Leadership, Spring 1969

Serious internal problems of the country, however, were in no way eased by this confrontation. The Communist Party leadership, mindful of the popular mood and anxious to maintain the support from the citizens, strove for a compromise which would permit the preservation of at least some essential features of the reform program, without too severely antagonizing the Soviet Union. Some concessions on the personal level appeared necessary to this end. Appointments and demotions made by the Fourteenth Party Congress in its emergency session had to be declared invalid. Several leading Central Committee and Party Presidium members resigned their functions in the first months after the invasion. On the other hand, until early spring, 1969, outspoken representatives of the conservative wing of the Party did not seem to have made many inroads into the controlling organs of the CPCS. In most cases, the seats vacated by the "liberals" were filled by moderate, rather than "dogmatic," elements; in some cases, Dubček's group was even able to eliminate some of its pro-Soviet opponents.

More serious than the danger of an eventual mass comeback of the conservatives appeared to be, early in 1969, the risk that some "progressive" Party leaders, induced by either unselfish or opportunistic motives, might lend themselves to misuse for Soviet purposes. The Kremlin, desirous to destroy the united front of Czechoslovak resistance, believed that a weak spot could be found in the Slovak communist movement where the memories of Antonín Novotný's unfortunate ethnic policy were still very much alive.

These considerations might have led the Soviets to place their confidence in the First Secretary of the Slovak CP Gustav Husák, hardly a "dogmatist" in the usual sense: He had opposed Novotný who jailed him for life in 1954, and after January, 1954, he was active in drafting the CPCS Action Program. The Soviets accepted him because his nationalism promised to lead to frictions between the Czechs and the Slovaks and thus weaken their solidarity.

The Soviets were determined to remove Dubček and to undo their loss of prestige in August, 1968, when the virtually unanimous popular support of Dubček frustrated their attempt to strip him of office. As a Czechoslovak ice-hockey victory sparked off anti-Soviet demonstrations all over Czechoslovakia in March, 1969, the U.S.S.R. found a pretext for accusing Prague leaders of incompetence and unwillingness to impose "normalization." Pressure by the Kremlin resulted in Dubček's yielding his post to Husák on April 17, 1969. Other shifts in high offices followed, including the ouster of the reformist Josef Smrkovský from the Party Presidium.

The Soviet threats of force were followed by a new, tighter control of the press, until a full advance-censorship was formally re-established. Although even this measure seemed unlikely to bring back the mood prevalent in the mass media before Novotný's fall, its results could be felt: Several reformist periodicals were stopped by either administrative decree or by their own voluntary decision, while the official Party press was put under close supervision by the Presidium.

In the late spring of 1969, while these lines are being written, it is difficult to foresee whether Soviet expectations as to the outcome of the CPCS leadership crisis will eventually be fulfilled. Psychologically the Soviets' success is indisputable. Dubček was an important symbol to his people, and the Soviets succeeded in demolishing this symbol. However, one cannot overlook that the real Dubček did not correspond to this popular image: circumstances rather than the strength of his personality made him a national hero. Thus his demotion may mean more in terms of prestige than of the CPSC's actual capacity to pursue its own policies.

The choice of Dubček for the First Party Secretary in January, 1968, was fortunate because he enjoyed confidence of both the Czechs and the Slovaks. In April, 1969, Husák seemed handicapped in this respect by his militant nationalist past which had estranged many Czechs from him. He also seemed less dedicated than Dubček to civic rights and freedoms, and less responsive to public opinion. These shortcomings might appear assets to the Soviets, but it is questionable whether Husák's strong personality will prove to Soviet advantage in the long run. In his first public speech as First Party Secretary, Husák said that the reforms initiated in January, 1968, would be continued. He also stated that his own past experience was a guarantee that the legal order would not revert to the conditions prevalent under Novotný.[18] Only the future can show whether the new leadership will be willing and able to follow with actions its verbal commitments.

[18] *Rudé Právo* (Prague), April 18, 1969.

EVALUATION, TRENDS, AND
PROSPECTS

In the modern history of Czechoslovakia, the main concern of the political élites has been to secure the country's independence, achieved after a generations-long struggle. This preoccupation became intensified by the German threat in the late thirties. The traumatic experience of the Munich crisis in 1938, which exposed the precariousness of the Western political and military guarantees, brought about a thorough revision of Czechoslovakia's self-image. The politically relevant strata of the population began to view the alliance with the Soviet Union as a vital necessity to Czechoslovakia. The respect which had to be paid to this most important ally hampered considerably the noncommunist majority in resisting the drive for power of the communists, whose adroit propaganda succeeded in identifying the interests of the Communist Party with those of the U.S.S.R. Thus the concern about national independence defeated its own purpose and became instrumental in the absorption of Czechoslovakia into the communist party-state system.

Two decades of communist rule in Czechoslovakia, the first and only economically developed country that communism has ever been able to conquer in its entirety, failed to provide a proof of validity of the predictions made by Marxist classics. Communism did not prove to be any more practicable in a highly industrialized Czechoslovakia, under the "mature" conditions postulated by dialectical and historical materialism, than it was in the "immature" economy of the 1917 Russia and in all other communist party states. The Czechoslovak experiment thus did not confirm the "orthodox" ideas of Marx and Engels as opposed to the "deviationist" ideas of Lenin and Stalin, but rather seemed to disprove both conceptions of the socialist revolution. In other words, Marxism in Czechoslovakia has not passed the field test. On the contrary, the Czechoslovak experience has shown that a country with a strong industrial and democratic tradition is even less suitable for communist methods of rule and economic organization than underdeveloped areas are.

In consequence of applying these methods with extraordinary rigidity for almost twenty years, the basic problems of the country were considerably aggravated. Czechoslovakia has always faced two major integration problems, one on the internal, national level and the other on the external, international level. In the first place, there was the need to overcome the chronic dichotomy between natural propensities toward close economic co-operation with its immediate neighbors, particularly with Germany, and the necessity to secure the country's existence and independence from eventual expansionist moves of the same neighbors. Equally serious has been the internal integration problem of accommodating two main ethnic elements, the Czechs and the Slovaks, in one state. Under the impact of communist policies between 1948 and 1967, the complexity and the urgency of these two crucial problems further increased.

The attempt to bring into harmony the economic

ties and the system of political and military alliances by channeling economic relations exclusively into the Central and Eastern European markets seriously disturbed Czechoslovak industry, distribution of its products, and foreign trade. The attempts at vertical economic integration, made in the course of the intensive socialist development period to modify Czechoslovak conditions to correspond to the Soviet model, as well as attempts at horizontal integration, undertaken during the thaw period in the form of the international socialist division of labor within the framework of the COMECON, brought only limited results. The international socialist division of labor, even in its actual, not too ambitious form, has increased rather than decreased the differences in industrial development between Czechoslovakia and most of the remaining communist party states. In short, the communist party-state system has not yet been able to integrate a foreign body of Czechoslovakia's type. Instead, the alien characteristics of the country have become even more pronounced, both in the political and in the economic spheres.

Internal integration of Czechoslovakia's two ethnic components was seriously obstructed by communist centralism prior to January, 1968. The peak of the drive aiming at the assimilation of the Slovaks was reached with the 1960 Constitution. Later, liberal and progressive elements in the CPCS became keenly conscious of the vital importance of this problem; however, their efforts were for a long time thwarted by the hostile attitude of the dogmatic leadership. Orthodox communism proved unable to contribute anything to the solution of either of the two basic questions of Czechoslovakia.

It was only after the removal of the orthodox group around Antonín Novotný that new approaches began to be considered by the CPCS. Czechoslovakia started openly to seek closer economic contacts outside the communist party-state system, restoring some of the partnership that had existed in Central and Eastern Europe in the pre-entry period. A far-reaching constitutional reform was prepared to satisfy the aspirations of the Slovak ethnic group and to loosen the centralist political and administrative pattern of government, inherited from Austria-Hungary and further solidified during the twenty years of communist regime. The "Czechoslovak way to socialism," professed by the leaders who succeeded Antonín Novotný, could be understood as an attempt to pursue policies which would be more in accordance with the vital national interests than the previous course, while respecting Czechoslovakia's affiliation with the communist party-state system. This proved to be more difficult than suspected by the reformists; though they often referred to the "historical" meaning of the decisions taken by the Communist Party following the January Plenum, it is unlikely that they were fully aware of how radical were the changes they had initiated. They seemed to be even less aware of the possible international consequences of these changes.

Until 1968, an unswerving reliance of the Czechoslovak Party on the Soviet Union and a firm adherence of Czechoslovakia to the communist party-state system belonged to the primary objectives of all leading teams of the CPCS. This loyalty had a special motivation. The Czechoslovak communist movement, unlike the parties in Yugoslavia, Albania, or China, did not come to power through its own efforts but thanks to a favorable international situation in which the domestic political forces had been reduced to a secondary role. Communism has remained largely an implanted organism in the national body. All communists prior to

1968 were conscious of this fact, and they saw therefore the Soviet power as the best guarantee of their own remaining in control if not of plain surviving. The Dubček team appeared less concerned about these things; most probably, the generation factor played here a prominent role, as the reformist leaders—mostly men around forty—had been brought up politically after the World War II and thus identified themselves with the Czechoslovak communist state rather than with the faraway Soviet Union, unlike their fathers in whose time the U.S.S.R. had been the only communist country and thus "the true fatherland of all socialists." Also, they seemed to take the communist order in Czechoslovakia more or less for granted, sufficiently strong to withstand the effects of the proposed reforms.

However, the risks involved in the process of the "democratization of socialism" and in the "return to progressive national traditions" were great. The comparisons which the Czechoslovak people have been able to make between the communist political and economic order and the order which had existed in a relatively recent past, always constituted a serious challenge to the regime. In the eyes of the politically minded non-communist majority, the democratic parliamentary system which had been in operation before the coup d'état of 1948 has remained a practical, workable alternative to communism. Consequently, there was a real possibility that a truly independent "Czechoslovak road to Socialism" would lead, sooner or later, to a truly democratic socialism, i.e., to a restoration, in one form or another, of the pre-communist political institutions. Such a turn of events would have put an end to the power monopoly of the communists, or, as it is formulated in the "dogmatic" language, to the leading role of the Party.

There is an evidence that the Czechoslovak reformist

leadership was determined to prevent this eventuality from happening. It was willing to go a long way toward making the experiment of democratized socialism work: It restored some basic conditions of classical democracy (the most important among these was the abolition of press censorship), but it would have probably never consented to reintroduction of a system with more than one independent political party. However, even if the group led by Alexander Dubček had had the opportunity to establish a new political order along these lines, it would have been a very precarious order. All historical experience has shown that human and civil rights are impossible to separate. The suspension of one devalues the effect of the other and, inversely, the full exercise of one right creates an irresistible pressure for granting all the remaining rights. It is very likely that a "compromise democracy," as envisaged by the Party after January, 1968, would have opened the door to new, much more radical, demands, both among the Party's rank-and-file members and among the noncommunist majority of the nation.

An equally strong, and possibly stronger, agent of change than the popular pressure for extension of specific civic freedoms was the necessity for economic reform. Indeed, Czechoslovak "revisionism" was primarily economic. It appeared much later and under completely different conditions from the "revisionism" in the neighboring countries, but it eventually proved to be more fatal to the old system of government than the most daring criticism of either the Marxist doctrine or of the communist ruling practices that had been voiced in 1956 and later in the communist world. Once under way, the New Economic Model, the concrete formulation of the reformist program, developed its own dynamics. It required a corresponding, far-reaching modification of the political structure. Moreover, the New Economic Model, with its notions of "market relations" and "material incentives," represented an implicit denial of the basic dogmas of Marxist economy. Its adoption testified to a profóund change in communist economic thought which had passed almost unnoticed—the recognition of the priority of the rights of the consumer. Czechoslovakia, more than any other communist party state, has subscribed to the value system of the consumer society. By accepting these yardsticks, even the most conservative elements in the Party became defenseless against attacks on the political order, waged from economic positions in the name of improving the general standard of living. It is highly probable that arguments based on a consumer society set of values would have also disarmed the last opposition against the emancipation of Czechoslovakia from its one-sided economic dependence upon the U.S.S.R.

Theoretically speaking, such development need not have necessarily meant an alienation of Czechoslovakia from the communist party-state system; we can easily imagine countries with entirely different inner political and economic structures to form a close alliance. However, the communist party-state system was definitely more than an alliance, and the inner transformation of any one among the member states would by itself already mean an estrangement. Whatever the intentions of the Dubček team were, the discrepancies in internal policies were bound to reflect upon the relations on international levels, chiefly because the power center in Moscow never ceased to consider the Soviet Union as the "leading socialist nation" whose wishes, if not example, were to be followed by the smaller party states in domestic matters also.

There could have been little doubt that the Soviets

would oppose an estrangement of Czechoslovakia from the community of communist nations. The preoccupation with the "purity" of communist teaching was not the only motive of this apprehensiveness. Plain power politics, too, played an important role. Czechoslovakia represented a vital element in the European northwestern tier of the communist system. Since the control over the eastern part of Germany has always ranked high on the list of Soviet priorities in the international arena, a friendly and reliable Czechoslovakia was essential to Moscow. Much depended on the interpretation of the terms "friendly" and "reliable," but historical experience indicated that, to the Kremlin leaders, these meant not only "pro-Soviet" but also "communist," that is, communist of the Soviet satellite type. Later events showed that those who had hoped to see a repetition of the "bridge" experiment of the immediate postwar period that would be made possible by a change in the international climate and a lessening of the Cold War tensions had wrongly assessed the true nature of the Soviet need for security.

It should not be overlooked that it was not a genuine need for security of the Soviet state, in the classical sense of the term, which had caused the Cold War, but Soviet drive for ideological expansion, and sometimes plain and straight Soviet imperialism. The fact is that it was the absorption into the communist party-state system of the countries liberated from the Nazi occupation by the Red Army and the attempts to incorporate additional territories either by subversion or by force that has created an alarm mood and need for security among the Western powers, who have responded by creating their own world-wide alliance as a counterpart of the Soviet super-bloc.

However, the Soviet feeling of insecurity does not

stem chiefly from a fear that the territories under communist control could be attacked by an outside enemy,
but from the knowledge of the instability of the communist system. Communism proved to possess a successful formula for seizing power. Yet, the economic and
political order which it attempted to build after the
seizure of power, revealed itself as not viable. The
power thus acquired could never be fully legitimized,
and any endeavor to modify established communist institutions has been perceived by the holders of this
power as an assault at the very substance of the regime.
It is the need for securing its own precarious internal
establishment that prompts the Soviet Union to obses-
sively seek external security for decades, and all other
considerations have always been subordinated to this
primary interest.

Under these conditions, the efforts of the Czechoslovak reformist leaders to maintain unchanged relations
with the U.S.S.R. and the other nations of the communist party-state system, while changing profoundly the
political and economic institutions of the country, appeared as a counterpart of the attempt to establish
democracy within a one-party set-up; both proved to be
problems comparable to squaring of the circle. The
Soviet Union could not remain indifferent to the
Czechoslovak reform movement because it postulated
an at least partial surrender of the Communist Party's
political monopoly and, consequently, imperiled the
whole communist system. This was probably the most
powerful motive of the Soviet intervention in Czechoslovakia in August, 1968. By forcing Czechoslovakia to
stop further progress in this direction, the Soviets believe they protect the tenuous foundations of world
communism.

However, this intervention—an act of grave, world-wide consequences—did not produce the result which had been expected, and failed to restore the "stable" conditions that had prevailed in Czechoslovakia before the fall of the Novotný clique. The Soviets did not realize how difficult it would be to attain their objective and how inadequate were the means they had chosen. They sensed the depth of the democratization movement and they feared its possible consequences, but they thoroughly misunderstood its origins. They were reluctant to admit that the movement started within the Communist Party and that it gained support of the noncommunist majority only later on; instead, they claimed that the CPCS "fell temporarily into the hands of enemies of socialism" and that the Czechoslovak proletariat became "disoriented." Soviet suspicion of a possible "counterrevolutionary conspiracy" in Czechoslovakia might have been quite genuine at their present level of understanding since the Soviet communists appeared unable to grasp the fact that the system they had installed in Czechoslovakia in 1948 collapsed by itself. The Czechoslovak communists did follow the Stalinist blueprint to the last detail and in the process of doing so became disillusioned about the usefulness of this Marxist design. What the contemporary Soviet leaders cannot comprehend is that communism in Czechoslovakia became a burnt-out shell and that their calls for "normalization"—which they understand as a restoration of the psychological climate prevalent in the first years of the Czechoslovak party state—are calls for the impossible.

This fact contains serious dangers for the time to come. The question is what the occupying power will do when it realizes that its goal to "normalize" the conditions in Czechoslovakia cannot be reached. Then another, far more drastic, intervention in Czechoslovakia's internal affairs might be chosen as the only possible solution. However, considering the nature of the problem, even such a step would hardly bring the desired result, except that it might further increase the tension between the people and the invaders. Also, the renewed use of naked force is unlikely to spark off new enthusiasm within the communist élites, whom long years of terror have rendered immune to this kind of incentive.

Yet an even more important question is whether the Soviets are capable of judging correctly the long-term effects of the intervention. The immediate effect of the invasion was the creation of a united front of the whole population, including the bulk of the membership of the Communist Party. In the long run, however, the fact that, at the moment of the intervention, the reformist leaders became symbols of national resistance does not hold any promise that communism could ever be rehabilitated in the eyes of the people. In the conditions created by the forceful Soviet step, the Communist Party of Czechoslovakia can survive politically—that is, maintain the popular backing—only if it consents to serve as the organizational basis of the Czech and Slovak anti-Soviet opposition. Yet if it accepts this role, it will perish as a distinct ideological movement in the amalgamating process of national reconciliation. If, on the other hand, it refuses to be the spokesman of the majority of the population, it will degenerate to the level of a tool of the foreign invader.

The Soviets might prefer a Czechoslovakia in the classical role of an occupied country with a puppet government, to the country which now, despite the presence of foreign troops, continues to manifest a will of its own. For some time to come, however, not even this choice will be available to the Soviets. Such a solution would probably require a direct take-over and continuous control of the most important government functions by Soviet military authorities—a situation comparable to that which existed under the nazi rule during World War II. It seems doubtful whether, at present, there would be any high-ranking communists, no matter how few, willing to collaborate and legitimize a regime of this kind. A Czechoslovak journalist observed wryly that the nation is just incapable of turning out any more collaborators. This observation is possibly more than a sample of grim humor. A totalitarian system—such as the Kremlin would like to see reinstated in Czechoslovakia—depends on the co-operation of countless volunteer informers who observe and report every move or idea as soon as it appears in their environment so that all unorthodoxy can be checked before it can grow dangerously strong. Without this volunteer, non-professional assistance, the general control mechanism is inoperative, no matter how perfect the professionally organized repressive network might be. Usually, only the Party members or sympathizers are sufficiently motivated to become informal volunteer helpers of the regime. At present in Czechoslovakia these volunteers are not available and cannot be expected to become available in the near future because the Czechoslovak elites became thoroughly and lastingly estranged from the Soviet Union.

The fact that the quasi-total population, including the rank-and-file members of the Party, came to see the Soviet Union as an enemy and to react to it in the manner in which Czechs and Slovaks reacted to the Austro-Hungarian Empire and to the German Third Reich, is a symptom of another indelible change brought about by the Soviet intervention. The reformist leaders in control are well aware of the new psychological climate and will probably make a serious effort to avoid comparison to the puppet governments of the German Protectorate of Bohemia and Moravia in the early forties. The Dubček government pledged several times its commitment to the Action Program of the CPCS, containing the basic principles of the reform movement. Even Gustav Husák, when he succeeded Alexander Dubček as Party First Secretary in April, 1969, promised that the leadership would "pursue firmly the policies of January."

The most important proof of Dubček's intentions was the enactment, in October, 1968, of the federalist constitutional reform. The hopes for viability of this political innovation were considerably increased by the fact that the Soviet intervention had restored in both ethnic groups the awareness of common destiny. Thus the Soviets, quite unwillingly, contributed to what may be a lasting solution of one of Czechoslovakia's main integration problems and, paradoxically, thus strengthened the ability of the country to resist the pressures from Moscow.

On the other hand, the federalization of the state might have been interpreted by the occupying power as an opportunity to play one ethnic group against another, the Slovaks against the Czechs preferably, because the former, being the smaller partner in the union, would be more likely to feel threatened or disadvantaged. Up to now, Soviet maneuvers to this end have not been very successful. They could become more effective in the future if the Slovak leaders came to appreciate more the idea of a formally independent Slovakia established with Soviet help than the chances of preserving at least some of the human and civil rights recently recovered within the framework of the Czechoslovak federation. Pressures to which the Slovak

169

communists were exposed following the Soviet intervention revealed that the nationalist-liberal alliance within the Slovak Party that had been effective in demolishing Antonín Novotný's power was by no means natural or automatic.

The Czechoslovak leaders must realize of course, that a modification of the constitutional structure of the state requires a corresponding logical modification of the organizational pattern of the Communist Party of Czechoslovakia. First steps toward this end, so far taken, have been rather timid and inconsistent. It will be one of the tests of how independent the team in control is, to see whether it will be able and willing to pursue the road of Party reform. This might not be easy because of the influence such a development might have upon the integrative relations within the communist party-state system. A federalized Czechoslovakia with a decentralized CPCS will represent, more than ever in the past, a foreign body among the strictly centralized nations and parties.

In the turmoil of the invasion, when all issues appeared to be of a political nature, the problem of economic reforms somehow receded into the background. However, not for a long time; the urgent need to remedy the economic shortcomings has been afresh recognized since then by the Czechoslovak leaders who know that their performance will be judged by the success of their economy. Theoretically, they have the choice between pursuing the New Economic Model along the lines contained in the Party's Action Program or taking any other measures apt to improve the general economic situation. In reality, their options are much narrower. Abandonment of the New Economic Model would by itself constitute a failure in the eyes of the people. Therefore, the government has to remain committed to the original plan also politically.

It is difficult to say how far the occupying powers might be willing to allow this course, as it is altogether uncertain what role the intentions of the Czechoslovak economic reformers played in the Soviet decision to intervene in Czechoslovakia. However, the Soviet Union also is interested in avoiding further economic setbacks which, as the Soviet leaders must know, would be viewed by the people of Czechoslovakia as a consequence of the invasion and further increase the anti-Soviet sentiment in the country. Though Moscow may still toy with the idea of holding back the aid for which the Dubček team applied before the intervention and releasing it only to some future, more pro-Soviet government in order to legitimize it by economic success, there might not be enough time for making this choice. While an alternative ruling team, more to the Soviet's liking, is slow in coming up, the economic difficulties can very quickly grow into serious proportions.

At the end of 1968, it became apparent that the new regime was determined to carry out the project of economic reform, albeit in a revised form. Government experts estimated that the first task would be to prevent the economic deterioration, while other, more ambitious goals could be pursued later on, particularly in the course of the Fifth Five-Year Plan (1971–1975). In February, 1969, the Prime Minister disclosed that Czechoslovakia obtained a substantial dollar loan from abroad, but withheld the information by whom this credit was granted, which would suggest that the loan was *not* awarded by the Soviet Union. This fact alone could indicate a measure of Czechoslovak independence in foreign trade matters. However, its real importance can be understood only in the wider context of Soviet economic strategy. The effects of this loan could be largely neutralized by the Soviets should they

171

succeed in increasing the already considerable proportion of the Soviet-Czechoslovak exchange of goods within the overall volume of Czechoslovak foreign trade, or in binding the economy of Czechoslovakia and other party states to the U.S.S.R. by means of further specialization within the framework of the COMECON.

Thus the Communist Party of Czechoslovakia, simultaneously exposed to the pressures from the Soviet Union and the exactly opposite pressures from the nation, continues to be in a very precarious situation. Since the yardsticks which it applies to the basic national problems are not necessarily identical with those adopted by the majority of the population for whom it came to speak in the exceptional conditions created by the Soviet invasion, it is unlikely that this apparent identity of interests should last for a long time. Hard pressed by the occupation power, the Czechoslovak communist leaders will probably settle in most cases for less than what the great majority of the people considers an acceptable minimum. That is why the gap between the nation and the Party will probably grow again, but with one essential difference: The political divide, this time, will no longer separate the Party as a whole from the noncommunist majority but it may rather run between the top officials and the rest of the people, including the rank-and-file members of the CPCS.

This transformation in the wake of the Soviet invasion is a fact of the most serious consequences for the communist party-state system. Since the bulk of the CP following had passed over into the nationalistic camp, the will of the Czech and Slovak people became again a potential political force. The Czechs and the Slovaks, whenever given the opportunity to decide about their own destiny in the future, can be expected to reject everything that the Soviet communism represents politically, economically, or morally. A new situation has been created, with Czechoslovakia joining those party states in which an eventual Soviet military pullout will bring a *certain and immediate* collapse of the Soviet-imposed system of government. In other words, the integration of Czechoslovakia into the communist system which had been supported by an ideologically motivated élite until August, 1968, has been maintained solely by the bayonets of the Red Army ever since then.

It is unlikely that the U.S.S.R., aware of the risks of evacuating the occupied territories in Central and Eastern Europe, will seriously consider such a move in the near future. The confrontation between Czechoslovakia and the occupation power will probably continue for a long time. The chances that a new, more adroit and imaginative policy of the West, adopting among other demands the removal of foreign troops from all countries—a demand which the Soviet propaganda had exploited for years but has to abandon now—would assist the striving for emancipation of nations in the communist party-state system, do not appear very great. It is characteristic for the Western frame of mind that the only concrete response to the invasion of Czechoslovakia was an increase in the combat readiness of the NATO forces, whereas a call for the dissolution of the military alliances would have been far more appropriate. The West seems to be too deeply committed to the policy of maintaining peace by preserving the balance between the two super-blocs. Moreover, the policy makers of the United States apparently believe that at least some of the major world issues can be settled in bilateral talks with the Soviet Union. This approach

173

suggests the often decried division of the world into the spheres of influence, implicitly agreed to at Yalta in 1945, which alone could justify the invasion in the crude terms of power politics. It rather enhances the international position of the U.S.S.R., in a situation where isolation and increasing moral and political pressure are the course to adopt, in order to make the intervention in Czechoslovakia as costly to the Soviets as possible. It is an almost tragic paradox that precisely at the moment when the policy of containment, initiated two decades ago, and that of "competitive coexistence" begin to bring fruit in the form of disintegration within the Soviet monolithic empire, the ghost of Yalta should thwart the results of twenty years of patient statesmanship and turn the Western powers into indirect accomplices in the prolonged enslavement of Central and Eastern Europe.

Thus the only hope for a tolerable solution of the "Czechoslovak problem" will depend on the Soviet Union itself for a long time to come, i.e., on a possible change in the leadership and/or the policies of the Kremlin. To overlook the tremendous difficulties and the depth of the necessary change in assessing the chances of such an event would mean to indulge in wishful thinking. While, before the invasion, it would have been essential for the Soviets to recognize that the "democratization" was the last opportunity to preserve communism in Czechoslovakia, it would have been equally essential to recognize that the conditions for a frutiful relationship between Czechoslovakia and the rest of the party states would become still more difficult to maintain after the intervention. Any realistic policy of Moscow must now take into account the total and permanent estrangement of the Czechs and the Slovaks from the Soviet Union and the party-state system. The possibilities of keeping Czechoslovakia within the communist system by other than violent means are almost nonexistent at present; the primary condition for doing so would be not less than the Soviet surrender of the "leading role," in both ideological and political matters. Already before August, 1968, the Soviets have proved unable to do this in regard to the Czechoslovak reform movement which does not seem to justify any optimism as to their ability to draw correct conclusions from the new situation. They can be even less expected to renounce their claim to being the supreme authority in communist matters, as such a step would imply a denial of the very principle which had justified the occupation of Czechoslovakia. Also, the new doctrine of "limited sovereignty of socialist states" formulated by Soviet politicians and ideologists after the invasion—a subject of vehement controversy within the international communist movement ever since—suggests that the Kremlin is not likely to revise its position on this question very soon.

The future handling of Czechoslovakia by the Soviet leaders will also depend, to a considerable extent, on their interpretation of the trends of international relations. Do they believe they stand on the threshold of a world communist revolution, where the primary task appears to be to further this revolution even at the cost of great sacrifices on the part of the nations already integrated in the party-state system? Or do they see communism passing through a period of crises, when the maximum goal is consolidation, if necessary at the cost of stagnation or even retreat from some already conquered areas? It would seem that the present group in control subscribes to the second, rather than to the first, theory; however, its position is not quite clear, if we only consider, for example, the effort spent in preparing another international communist assembly. Both these interpretations contain risks of a sharpening of the conflict as well as promises of a possible easing of dangerous tensions in Central and Eastern Europe.

The expectations of an imminent enlargement of the area under communist control might prompt the center of power in Moscow to try enforcing discipline among the party states by all available means; yet, on the other hand, it might strengthen the concern of Soviet leaders for an attractive image of communism in the noncommunist world and discourage an indiscriminate use of force in intra-bloc relations. In this eventuality, the opinion of communist parties which cannot be ruled directly from Moscow would gain weight and, as experience has shown, would favor a settlement more acceptable to Czechoslovakia. As for the Soviet Union's other possible interpretation of current development trends, namely, that these are the times of test for the communist party-state system, it could move the Soviets to try to bring about a full alignment of Czechoslovakia, regardless of consequences, or it might also induce the Kremlin leaders to review their relations to Czechoslovakia in terms of the costs and benefits and, eventually, to resign themselves to the special situation in that country. This latter alternative would be realized if the U.S.S.R., in the interest of consolidating its position in Europe, reduced the *sine qua non* area under its immediate physical control to the western tier of the system, namely to East Germany and, by implication, to Poland.

Similarly ambivalent conclusions, suggesting two possible different policies on Czechoslovakia, could be drawn by the Soviets should another serious conflict arise within the communist party-state system. Such might be the clash between the U.S.S.R. and the

Chinese People's Republic that resulted in small-scale military confrontations in March, 1969, and in formalization of the schism by the subsequent Chinese Communist Party Congress. Further increase in tensions with China might induce the Kremlin either to tighten its grip on the occupied, unreliable Czechoslovakia or to try pacifying this country by concessions for its greater independence. The action of Moscow in connection with anti-Soviet demonstrations in Prague in April, 1969, might have been prompted by concern over a possible weakening of the European component in the communist party-state system in the face of the threat to the Soviet power in the Far East.

Although the Soviets may adopt either a "tough" or a conciliatory line in any situation, whatever they do will bear upon the vital interests of world communism. The current crisis, of which the conflict with Czechoslovakia is but one dramatic symptom, seems to indicate that only a more balanced and sophisticated approach could preserve world communism as a somewhat meaningful concept. Soviet leaders do not seem to realize that cohesion of the world communist movement depended in the past on selfless, ideologically motivated elites in control of communist parties and party states. These elites followed voluntarily Soviet guidelines and were genuinely loyal to the "Fatherland of Socialism." However, in almost all communist countries, elite groups underwent a radical change during the "thaw" in the fifties and sixties. Pressure cannot make up for their evaporated enthusiasm. On the contrary, indiscriminate use of force only increases the risk of new and more dangerous conflicts.

The communist party-state system, designed as a strait jacket with the purpose of preventing all reform, is doomed; pluralism is the price of its plain

177

survival. Relative stability of the situation in Central and Eastern Europe—and thus tolerable conditions of existence for Czechoslovakia—will depend on the willingness of the Soviet center of power to pay this price. If the future of the communist world—and, indeed, of the whole world—is not to be fraught with incalculable perils, the Soviet Union must not conceive its security as security from change.

SELECTED BIBLIOGRAPHY

The Pre-Entry Period

Diamond, William. *Czechoslovakia between East and West.* London: Stevens, 1947.

Griffith, William E. *Communism in Europe.* Vol. 2, Part 2, (prepared by Zdeněk Eliáš and Jaromír Netík). Cambridge: The M.I.T. Press, 1966.

Kann, Robert A. *A Multinational Empire—Nationalism and National Reform in the Habsburg Monarchy 1848 1918.* New York: F. A. Praeger, 1950.

Seton-Watson, Hugh. *Eastern Europe between the Wars, 1918–1941.* London: Archon Books, 1962.

Wheeler, John Bennet. *Munich—Prologue to Tragedy.* London: Macmillan, 1963.

The Entry and Post-Entry Periods

Friedman, Otto: *The Break-up of Czech Democracy.* London: Gollancz, 1950.

Gadourek, Ivan. *The Political Control of Czechoslovakia; a Study in Social Control of a Soviet Satellite State.* Leiden: H. E. Stenfert Kroesse, 1953.

Korbel, Josef: *The Communist Subversion of Czechoslovakia, 1938–1948.* Princeton: Princeton University Press, 1959.

Ripka, Hubert. *Czechoslovakia Enslaved.* London: Gollancz, 1950.

Skilling, H. Gordon. *The Governments of Communist East Europe.* New York: Thomas Y. Crowell, 1966.
Táborský, Eduard. *Communism in Czechoslovakia, 1948–1960.* Princeton: Princeton University Press, 1961.
U.S. Congress. *Communist Takeover and Occupation of Czechoslovakia.* Washington: 1954.
Zinner, Paul: *Communist Strategy and Tactics in Czechoslovakia.* London: Pall Mall, 1963.

Works Dealing With Special Aspects

Feierabend, Ladislav. *Agricultural Co-operatives in Czechoslovakia.* Washington: Mid-European Studies Center, 1952.
Lazarcik, Gregor. *The Performance of Socialist Agriculture—A Case Study of Production and Productivity in Czechoslovakia 1934–1938 and 1946–1961.* New York: International Financial Research, 1963.
Operations Research Office, The Johns Hopkins University. *Czechoslovakia: An Area Manual.* 2 vols. Baltimore: The Johns Hopkins Press, 1955.
Thad-Alton, Paul. *Czechoslovak National Income and Product 1947–48 and 1955–56.* New York: Columbia University Press, 1962.
Zaubermann, Alfred. *Industrial Progress in Poland, Czechoslovakia and Eastern Germany.* London: Oxford University Press, 1964.